The Developing Child

Recent decades have witnessed unprecedented advances in research on human development. Each book in The Developing Child series reflects the importance of this research as a resource for enhancing children's well-being. It is the purpose of the series to make this resource available to that increasingly large number of people who are responsible for raising a new generation. We hope that these books will provide rich and useful information for parents, educators, child-care professionals, students of developmental psychology, and all others concerned with childhood.

Jerome Bruner, University of Oxford
Michael Cole, Rockefeller University
Barbara Lloyd, University of Sussex
Series Editors

The Psychology of Childbirth

Aidan Macfarlane

Harvard University Press
Cambridge, Massachusetts

Library of Congress Cataloging in Publication Data
Macfarlane, Aidan, 1939-
  The psychology of childbirth.
  (The Developing child)
  Bibliography: p.
  Includes index.
  1. Childbirth—Psychological aspects.
2. Infant psychology. 3. Mother and child.
I. Title [DNLM: 1. Labor. 2. Maternal
behavior. 3. Prenatal care. 4. Parent—Child
relations. 5. Child development. WQ200 M143p]
RG658.M3   155.4'22   76-51311
ISBN 0-674-72105-5 (cloth)
ISBN 0-674-72106-3 (paper)

This book is dedicated to Elizabeth, Magnus, and Tamara.

Contents

	Prologue	1
1	Life Before Birth	5
2	Social and Psychological Factors	15
3	The Delivery: When and Where	23
4	Pain and Relief	33
5	The First Minutes	51
6	What the Baby Knows	73
7	Mother and Child: Separation	99
8	Mother and Child: Socialization	115
	Epilogue	125
	References	129
	Suggested Reading	135
	Index	137

The
Psychology of
Childbirth

Prologue

The complex social and behavioral changes within our society frequently seem to defeat the analytic endeavors of psychologists, sociologists, economists, and philosophers. It is, however, fortunate that the world is also populated with those who are unable to accept the limitations of science and scientific methods, people for whom the inability to quantify emotion, mysticism, and change still provides a certain joy and satisfaction.

One of the recent major social changes for which it is difficult to assign causes has been the reassessment of the position of women within our society and of their role in childbearing. From the standpoint of medical management, childbirth has been mainly a male prerogative, with the result that the physical aspects of birth have been better managed than the emotional ones. It would be difficult to deny the enormous benefits in terms of decrease in death and damage to babies and mothers which medical advances have brought about. Therefore I frequently emphasize in this book that it is only possible to examine the psychological aspects of childbirth in the knowledge that both mother and baby have an optimal chance of survival.

The reduction of the deathrate among mothers and their babies, however, has meant more and more interference in the processes of birth. Mothers now having babies are considered "patients in hospitals" rather than human beings who go through normal physiological and psychological developments. To a certain extent we seem to have reached a point of diminishing returns: increasing interference provides less and less in terms of improved outcome. In spite of lip service paid to the idea that psychological and physiological changes are so linked that

1

changes in one area do not occur without changes in the other, little use is made of the connection. Nevertheless, psychological factors can be used both to predict where trouble may occur in pregnancy and birth and to improve the quality of the experience.

Childbirth is an emotional and immeasurably complex aspect of existence, and the experience means a great deal to the individuals involved, both at the time itself and later. Thus recent research into psychology and human behavior can give insights that do not detract from the mystery of birth and increase our knowledge of the exciting possibilities of variation and influence. Nothing in this book is meant to indicate that there is a right or wrong way in childbirth. I simply want to examine some of the recent research findings in an area that may be of interest to those having babies or those helping in the processes of childbirth. None of this information is infallible. The psychology of childbirth is itself still in its infancy and faces extraordinarily difficult methodological problems in disentangling the many possible causes and effects involved in pregnancy and delivery. Thus the information that has been gained should be approached carefully—and it can be accepted or rejected as it seems to respond to the individual's own sensibilities, knowledge, and experience. In some cases it may provide a degree of insight, and in others it may meet with outright rejection.

Although my book is concerned with childbirth, birth is of course only one part of a continually unfolding relationship from conception onward, first between the baby and the mother and, after birth, between the child, the mother, the father, and the environment in general. Because of this, the chapters are chronologically ordered, dealing first with the baby's experiences in the uterus and with the mother's psychology during pregnancy. After these come the delivery and the parents' first reactions to the newborn baby. We move then to the way in which the baby perceives the outside world and how he may influence and be influenced by his new environment.

Between chapters are transcripts of actual deliveries. I video-recorded them in the labor room, as part of a research project on the first meetings of mothers and their babies. Many of the questions raised in this book are related to one question: Does delivery have any long-term effect? Still it must be emphasized that we do not spend our whole lives worrying about the long-term effects of what we are doing. Rather we are more often concerned with the immediate quality and satisfaction of the experience. This must surely apply to childbirth.

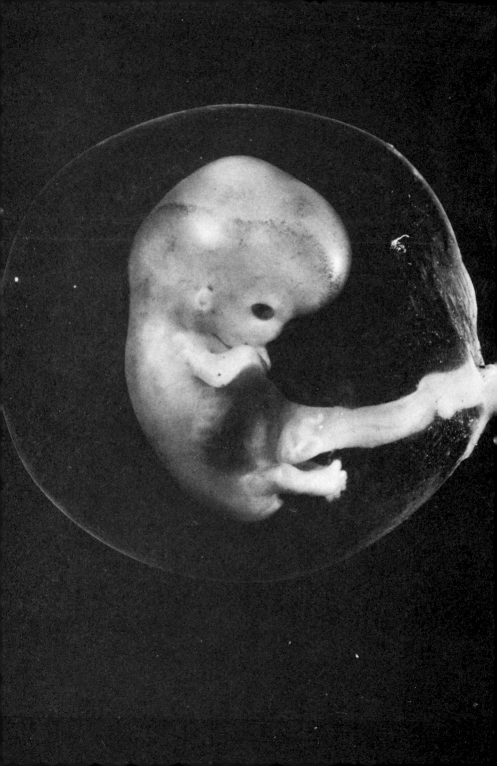

1 / Life Before Birth

It seems extraordinary that astrologers base a horoscope containing predictions for a whole lifetime on the exact time and date of delivery—a time and date that today are more frequently chosen by the obstetrician than by fate.

In China and Japan, a child is considered to be one year old at birth; the child's individual existence during his* development within the mother's uterus is thereby acknowledged from the moment of conception. The importance of this period was well noted by physician and philosopher Sir Thomas Browne, who in 1642 wrote: "Every man is some months older than he bethinks him, for we live, move, have being, and are subject to the actions of the elements and the malice of diseases, in that other world, the truest Microcosm, the womb of our mother." To this the poet Samuel Taylor Coleridge added in 1802, in the margin of Browne's book, "Yes—the history of man for the nine months preceding his birth would probably be far more interesting and contain events of greater moment, than all the three score and ten years that follow it."

The belief that events can influence the unborn child—and may be caused by such factors as magic, the gods, and the planets, or by the infant's own actions, or by events affecting the pregnant woman—has been held through all of recorded history in all cultures. In fact, even today Lyall Watson in *Supernature* gives a very plausible argument for the influence of the planets on human development.[1] Hippocrates in 400 B.C. and Serenus in

---

*Assuming that the baby is male has no special significance, but it helps avoid confusion with his (or her) mother.

5

the first century A.D. expressed a firm belief that the pregnant woman influenced her unborn child, and a thousand years ago the Chinese were running prenatal clinics, not so much in the interest of physical well-being as to ensure tranquility in the mother and, through her, in the baby. In the Middle Ages, however, magic and demons were believed to hold sway, and midwives were thought to be witches.

Philosophies changed, and by the fifteenth century Leonardo da Vinci could see direct links once more between mother and child: "The things desired by the mother are often found impressed on parts of the child who the mother carried at the time of the desire. So it is concluded that one and the same soul governs the two bodies, and the same body nourishes both." Also current at this time was the agreeable notion that the mother's and father's "imaginings" at conception would influence the outcome of the pregnancy. Since it is possible to assume that on the whole sexual intercourse is a pleasant experience, then most of the outcomes should be good.

The body of scientific opinion during the last century and the earlier part of this one promoted the idea of the uterus as a fortress, impregnable to anything other than sperm. The uterus was imaged as a kind of mausoleum entombing the fetus within it. There was no internal or external stimulation of any kind until, at the end of nine months, life suddenly burst out.

But, as early as 1889, Hirsh had drawn up an impressive list of substances moving from the blood of the mother to the blood of the child across the placental barrier—including opiates, tobacco, and ether; and L. W. Sontag in the 1930s showed how smoking and loud noises could affect the heartrate of a baby in the uterus.[2] The full significance of the interaction between mother and fetus was finally realized at the time of the thalidomide disaster of the 1960s. There are now over 1500 substances that are known to have an adverse effect on the developing fetus. Many of these are drugs, which can cross the placenta rapidly from mother to child. These drugs may have a beneficial effect on the mother (also a deleterious one), but often they have disastrous effects on the embryo. Maternal malnutrition, X-rays, and smoking are among other harmful factors. Mothers who smoke have an increased chance of producing a small or sick baby, and more directly it has been shown that when a pregnant woman smokes the breathing movements of the fetus are modified for up to an hour after the cigarette.

In its turn, the fetus has an effect on the mother's physiology, as so nicely summed up by Frank Hytten: "The fetus is an egoist, and by no means an endearing and helpless little dependent as his mother may fondly think. As soon as he has plugged himself into the uterine wall he sets out to make certain that his needs are served, regardless of any inconvenience he may cause. He does this by almost completely altering the mother's physiology, usually by fiddling with her control mechanisms."[3]

We all live in a constantly changing world, and we ourselves have to change and adapt to our environment, as well as change and adapt the environment. The internal changes that occur within us are of many different kinds, chemical, mechanical, physiological, psychological. The baby, a single cell at conception, goes through all the inconceivably complex developments to become, at nine months of age in the uterus, as sophisticated as most animals ever are in a lifetime. He has been surrounded by the changing world of his mother's body, which he himself has also been influencing by his own existence. What can we find out about what the world is like to a baby inside his mother?

SOUND IN THE UTERUS

A baby cannot voice his feelings while in the uterus or later remember them to tell us what they were like. Nor can we directly observe his behavior there. We can only use what mothers tell us about their babies' behavior, make inferences by observing babies born long before they have reached full term, or use highly sophisticated equipment like the ultrasonic scanner.

So we must try to derive a good deal about the baby's behavior in the uterus from relatively few observed facts. For instance, if we put a loudspeaker on the tummy of a pregnant mother and play five seconds of, say, Elvis Presley turned up to almost deafening loudness, we would probably notice, if the mother is getting on toward the end of pregnancy, that each time the sound is turned on, the baby becomes more active. But the baby's reaction might depend on how quickly the music is turned up, how loud it gets, what vibration frequencies are being used, how long the sound lasts, or all of these. One can certainly say there is something about that particular noise that makes the baby more active, though of course we can say nothing about how he "feels" about the sound.

Ever-observant mothers have long been aware that, when they attend a concert or a pop festival, or simply find themselves standing near a door when it slams or near a passing train, their babies tend to become more active in the uterus. In fact, many mothers attribute later sensitivity to sound after birth to such occurrences. The first experimental work done on the effect of sounds and vibrations on the unborn child was carried out by Sontag.[4] In the 1930s he applied a vibrator, producing 120 vibrations a second, to the tummies of eight pregnant women during the last three months of pregnancy and found a marked increase in the babies' movements each time the vibrator was turned on, as well as a marked increase in the babies' heartrate.

It was not clear from this whether the baby was reacting directly to the sound across the tummy wall of the mother or whether his reaction came as a result of the mother herself feeling or hearing the sound. If she suddenly heard a startling sound, she would become more alert, causing a change in the amount of certain hormones excreted in her body; this might in turn contract her uterus slightly, increasing the pressure in the fluid around the baby and making him move. The question was decided by transmitting high-frequency sounds through a vibrator attached to the mother's tummy wall while, at the same time, having her wear headphones into which another sound was played continuously. The high-frequency sounds played for the infant could not be felt or heard by the mother. This method revealed that the babies were indeed reacting directly to the sound and vibration and also that this reaction occurred within five seconds of the sound's being turned on.[5] It also showed that babies responded to low frequencies—so low that they cannot be appreciated by the human ear—which must have been acting at some point on the babies' bodies. There is evidence that sounds the mother hears with her own ears will alter the baby's heartbeat, although not until much more time has elapsed than the five seconds noted when the baby was stimulated directly across the tummy wall.

But what happens to the sound as it passes across the mother's body and through the fluid that surrounds the baby? To answer this question, researchers inserted very small microphones through the cervix into the uterus to lie alongside the baby's head and record the sounds that come in from the outside.[6] Recordings from these microphones showed, much to everyone's surprise, that there is a very loud noise going on all the time in the uterus. It is a rhythmical whooshing sound, punctuated by the tummy rumbles of air passing through the mother's stomach. The pulsating noise keeps exact time with her heart and is due to blood flowing through her uterus. It turns out that almost all external noises are muted as they pass across the mother's body and through the amniotic fluid, and only extremely loud noises ever exceed the rhythmical sound the baby hears all the time.

The fact that babies are exposed to this sound in the uterus is not without its own significance, for even after birth they do seem to carry some kind of memory of life inside the uterus. Lee Salk noticed that mothers tend to hold their babies on the left side rather than the right (whether they were left- or right-handed), and he noted that most classical paintings of mother and child also show the infant on the left.[7] He proposed that this is because, when held on the left, the head of the baby is close to the mother's heart and that the sound of the heartbeat is comforting. He therefore looked at two groups of a hundred normal babies after birth. To one group he played a recording of an adult heartbeat of 80 beats a minute for four days. The other group had no heartbeat sound. At the end of the four days the heartbeat group had gained more weight and cried significantly less than the other group. Salk also played heartbeats at 120 beats a minute to a third group of babies, but they became so upset that he immediately had to stop the sound. More recently some Japanese pediatricians extended Salk's techniques by making a recording of the noise in the uterus and playing it to babies aged from birth to fourteen days. This sound had a marked calming effect, though I cannot help believing that it must be infinitely nicer being cuddled by mother than lying in a plastic crib listening to a recording of an anonymous uterus.

MOVEMENTS IN THE UTERUS

A baby makes several different kinds of movements in the uterus. First there are those in response to having some part of his body touched. Second there are those he makes spontaneously. Last there are movements of the chest, which seem to be breathing.

Movements in response to touch have mainly been observed in babies born very prematurely. But self-stimulation also occurs in the uterus: the baby is capable of touching parts of his body with his hands or feet, and the umbilical cord must also come into contact with his body and limbs. He makes many so-called reflexive movements: some away from the "touch," as if he were programmed to avoid it as harmful. Later in development these reflexes may become reversed, as if he were seeking to explore the touch.

At six weeks after conception the baby is about 2.5 centimeters long (almost one inch), and at this time his hands are held close to the mouth. If the hands touch the area around his mouth, he turns his head away and opens his mouth. Later, instead of turning away from the hand, he turns his head toward it and may even put a finger into his mouth. (Finger sucking is well known to occur in the uterus.) This turning also occurs after the baby has been born, and is called the rooting reflex.

At nine weeks after conception the baby's hand is well enough formed so that, if the palm of the hand is touched, he will bend his fingers; at twelve weeks the fingers and thumb will close. Pressure at the base of his thumb will also cause him to open his mouth and move his tongue. By twenty-five weeks the baby's grasp is strong enough to support the weight of his body.

At nine weeks a touch on the sole of the foot makes the baby curl his toes or straighten them out in a fan, as he bends his leg at the knee and hip to remove the foot from the touch. Walking and crawling motions also develop as a response to various positionings the baby finds himself in, and it is thought that these reflexes may enable him to get into the right position to be born.

At eleven weeks the baby is able to swallow, and a cycle of circulation is set up as he swallows some of the surrounding amniotic fluid and then pees it back out.

Mouth movements also show that the baby has the means to produce many sophisticated facial expressions, such as smiles and laughs. Smiles have been noted in babies born thirty-three weeks after conception, and even smaller fetuses have been seen to look pleased or distressed. But we still don't know whether at this stage these expressions accompany actual emotions.

A baby certainly makes spontaneous movements by seven weeks of intrauterine life, but most mothers will not feel their babies moving until between sixteen and twenty-six weeks. (Mothers are very good at telling when their babies are moving, for even when one uses electronic equipment to measure movements, the mother is almost as accurate.) Separate types of movements have been identified. There are slow, squirming movements, which increase during the course of pregnancy. Then there are sharp kicks, increasing in frequency up to the seventh month and then decreasing. Last there are small rhythmic hiccough-like movements, which occur at a low constant rate from the fifth to the ninth month of pregnancy. The amount of each activity varies enormously from one baby to another. Some of the movements follow cyclical variations that may be associated with the different states of sleep the baby goes through in the uterus. These states seem to coincide with the mother's sleep patterns; before birth they appear to be hormonally controlled, but the matching continues even after delivery.

I have already described how the baby may be affected by loud noises. Sontag recorded fetal movement in a group of mothers over several months and showed that the babies' activity increased when the mothers were under emotional stress.[8] If the emotion was intense but brief, there was only a transitory increase in activity, but with emotional upsets that lasted for longer periods of time there was a prolonged increase, up to ten times the normal level. The mothers also reported feeling increased movements when they themselves felt particularly tired.

A baby also makes breathing movements toward the end of pregnancy. Since at this stage he is surrounded by fluid, these are obviously not absolutely comparable to breathing after birth. Reports of these movements have been made by mothers for many years, and some have even noticed rhythmical movements of their own tummy wall! The breathing occurs about 70 percent of the time and may be punctuated by sighing or hiccoughing. It is still debatable whether some of the movements of the baby's chest represent his attempts to cry.

So we know that babies in the uterus are capable both of responding to touch and of producing spontaneous movement.

We cannot yet tell, though, how much of this movement is necessary for normal muscle development, or how much the fetus is learning about his own actions as he kicks his way around the uterus.

SEEING IN THE UTERUS

The muscles for moving the eye and the actual system for seeing develop very early on in pregnancy, and in the uterus the baby makes eye movements both in response to his changing positions and—as he will throughout life—during dreaming sleep. Not surprisingly, very little is actually known about what or how much the fetus sees. There is some evidence that toward the end of pregnancy the uterus and the mother's tummy wall get so stretched that some light does get through to become diffused in the amniotic fluid; it would look like the glow we see through a hand held over the end of a flashlight. If this is so, then the baby may go through periods of light and dark corresponding to the degree of light the mother is exposed to.

Babies born seven months after conception, when given a test with a single flash of light, do show changes in their brain-wave patterns, and at about this time their pupils begin to react to light. Babies can also be quieted with a repeatedly flashing light, at about 80 flashes a minute, even though they have had no previous experience of it—thus they seem to be born with a sensitivity to light rhythms.

The baby in the uterus lives in a warm, noisy, and maybe pink-tinted world, cushioned by surrounding fluid. He is mobile enough to turn somersaults and suck his finger should he so desire (if desire is a word one can use of a baby at this stage). The fluid will, from time to time, give him a gentle squeeze as the uterus contracts. Many influences are at work within this small world. The external environment—be it the far-distant planets or the more immediate social, cultural, and physical environment of the mother—plays a part, directly or through the mother. And the baby himself generates changes, as he moves, swallows, pees, and touches. With all of this, however, he is also always developing so that he can organize and respond to a very much more social world than he has ever experienced within the uterus.

2 / Social and Psychological Factors

In the physical sense there are only two ways of having a baby, vaginally or by cesarean section, but beyond this each and every birth is as individual as the woman herself who gives birth. There are no rights and wrongs, just differences, and in this chapter I want to outline some of the studies that have been made to explain the differences.

Influences on the outcome of a pregnancy and delivery begin at the time of the mother's own conception. The genes she inherits from her parents, her own development inside the uterus with all its complex changes, the hazards of her own delivery, her social and biological experiences during infancy, childhood, and adolescence—all form the basis for her mental and physical health as an adult. There are many other factors as well, such as where she lives, the people she grows up with, her social and economic status. All these affect, among other things, her experience of giving birth and bringing up her own children.

Most of the studies mentioned here have been carried out in Great Britain and the United States, and it is interesting in passing to speculate why certain cultures put emphasis on certain aspects of psychological research rather than on others (for instance, there is a great deal of interest in England on the influence of social-class differences). And a warning is needed here: because of the ever-changing intricacy of human nature, psychological studies on the same subject often fail to get the same results. This is in no way surprising, since it is impossible to ensure that all those people taking part in the study are exactly alike except with respect to the factor under study. It might help research if one could use a single mold to turn out a few thousand exact replicas of human beings, and then look at the effect on childbirth of, say, giving half of them a standardized lousy marriage. However, thanks to God or evolution, we are each and every one of us at least a little different from the next.

SOCIAL CLASS

Using the concept of social class to categorize portions of a population according to occupation began around 1910. It was expedient but perhaps unfortunate that it was the policy then to put women into different social classes according to their husbands' occupation, even if they had occupations of their own. To a large extent this method continues today.

The usual method of classification defines five different classes by occupation: professional; intermediate (for instance, teachers and managers); skilled, manual, or nonmanual; partly skilled; and unskilled.[1] Now social class is an abstract term—it only tells you what category someone's occupation puts him in, and nothing about what particular circumstance (say poor nutrition or heavy smoking) might make a difference because it is a class difference. As a research tool it has been likened to a doctor's thermometer, which can indicate that a problem exists but not actually what the problem is.

In England and Wales in 1911, it was decided to see how many children born to people in each of these five different class-occupations died in the first month of life. The results showed that, the lower your class, the greater the chance that your baby would die. In those days the deathrate for babies and mothers was high, whereas today, after great medical advances, only about 17 babies in every 1000 dies in the period around birth. Nevertheless, the same relationship between classes exists: more babies born to lower-class families die than those born to upper-class families. This is a strong indication that it is not just better and more accessible medical care that makes the difference. What is determined by belonging to a certain social class? Probably what you eat, where you live, how much attention you pay to your health, and much more. Differences in class seem to be related to significant differences in the birthweight too, and also in the incidence of congenital abnormalities. Social class is even the best predictor of a child's mental and physical development by the age of twelve. But research has only begun to explore these questions.

Other social factors that seem to affect biological and psychological outcomes include illegitimacy and prenuptial conception, the mother's age, the number of her previous children, her health and physique, and her work during pregnancy. Also important are smoking and drugs, stress and shock, the use of obstetric services, maternal nutrition, and so on. The very incidence of many of these factors as well may be significantly different from class to class.

THE PSYCHOLOGY OF THE MOTHER

A large number of psychological tests have been devised to assess certain variables in a woman's attitudes toward pregnancy. These include her concept of herself as a mother, her general psychosocial adjustment, her mental stability and familial-social adjustment, her notions of femininity. It has been the practice in psychology to try to relate such factors both to upsets in reproductive processes and also to variations within the norm.

Abnormalities of pregnancy and delivery. Habitual spontaneous abortion (miscarriage) has been the subject of extensive psychological research.[2] Tests given to women who have a history of abortion generally differentiate between those with physical diseases that cause the abortions and those without. In one study, both these groups scored quite differently from a control group in which there was no history of aborting. But another study reported that women who habitually aborted were confused over their sexual identity and lacking in support from their social environment. In two other studies, it was found that the cure rate in preventing further spontaneous abortion, by means of psychotherapy, was around 80 percent as compared with a cure rate of 26 percent in a group of aborters not so treated.

Nausea and vomiting would seem to be obvious candidates for psychoanalytic interpretation as disgust or rejection of the pregnancy. There is evidence, however, that the biochemical changes taking place at the beginning of a normal pregnancy do in fact lower a woman's threshold to nausea and vomiting. A study by S. Rosen, in which he interviewed fifty-four women in the first twelve weeks of pregnancy to assess emotional stress, found that heavy stress was present in all of the eighteen women with severe vomiting; where the amount of vomiting differed with subsequent pregnancies, this too could be correlated with the amount of stress in each of the pregnancies.[3] In yet another study, no relationship was found between vomiting during pregnancy and neurotic symptoms, sexual functioning, attitudes toward pregnancy, emotionally disturbing events, or an extroversion score. To date, then, there has been no conclusive evidence that vomiting during pregnancy is influenced by emotional factors.

The studies on prematurity are unfortunately mainly retrospective—that is, the psychological tests were done after the baby had been born.[4] Therefore, though the tests do show differences between the mothers of full-term babies and those of premature babies, these differences may be the result of having a small and vulnerable baby and have little to do with the reasons why the baby was born prematurely. The role of psychological factors in bringing about premature labor is still uncertain.

Toxemia during pregnancy, marked by hypertension and swelling, has been one of the hardest medical problems to solve. There is an apparent link between high blood pressure and anxiety and stress in people of all conditions, and so toxemia may have a psychosomatic basis. This is not immediately borne out by research, although there is a study by A. Coppen in which he looked at fifty women with toxemia and fifty without. He found significant differences in the two groups in their attitude toward pregnancy and the onset of menstruation; in premenstrual tension; in sexual adjustment; in incidence of vomiting; neuroticism; relation to siblings; and in emotionally disturbing events experienced during pregnancy.[5] Other studies have not uncovered such connections.

There seems to be a relation between anxiety, overt or covert, and the length of labor. Uterine dysfunction may also be associated with concealed anxiety. Harry Bakow found that mothers who were anxious during pregnancy and who expressed more concern over the course of their pregnancy more often had babies who got into distress at delivery.[6] Various more recent studies suggest that women likely to have complications during childbirth are those who during pregnancy manifested a negative attitude to the pregnancy, showed concern for the condition of the child, saw their employment as being disrupted, listed a greater number of contacts with women who had complicated pregnancies, and described their own mother's health as poor.

These, then, are the results of a few of the studies, but we can see how conflicting they are. Still, the value of all this research is that obstetrics as a whole greatly benefits by any method available that can predict which mothers will have trouble during pregnancy and delivery and which will not. If he has a good method of prediction, an obstetrician can concentrate his energies on the problem mothers and allow the others to deliver without interference, perhaps even at home. It may be that psychological testing in combination with routine medical tests will ultimately improve predictability.

Variations in normal pregnancy and delivery. Psychoanalysis has interpreted the role of normal pregnancy in the life of women in two ways. One interpretation is based on the idea of pregnancy as a crisis, an abnormal state of health which only returns to normal sometime after delivery. The alternative view is that pregnancy and delivery are part of the fuller normal development of a woman.

In support of the former theory, a number of researchers have produced evidence that indicates increased neuroticism in pregnant women. A study by P. A. Chapple and W. D. Furneaux tested women twice during pregnancy, on an introversion-extroversion scale and on a neuroticism scale.[7] They found that as pregnancy progressed the introverted women tended to become more neurotic, the extroverted women less neurotic. Pregnancy, they concluded, acts as a nonspecific stress and the response of women varies according to their personalities.

The view of the birth of a child as a normal stage in female development is well presented by Dana Breene in *The Birth of a First Child.*[8] She set out to test the idea that the biological and psychological event of becoming a mother activates processes that can be "adaptive or maladaptive." She intensively studied fifty women having first babies, using questionnaires, interviews and data collected from obstetricians, as well as formal psychological testing. The results, as one might expect from a study of this kind, were complex, but she holds that "those women who are most adjusted to childbearing are those who are less enslaved by the experience, have more differentiated, more open appraisals of themselves and other people, do not aspire to be the perfect selfless mother which they might have felt their own mother had not been, but are able to call on a good mother image with which they can identify, and do not experience themselves as passive, the cultural stereotype of femininity."

Emotions and the baby's behavior. As we have seen, there is evidence that the mother's emotions during pregnancy may influence the behavior of the child both in the uterus and after birth. Bakow's work showed that infants who were more alert in their responses when tested after birth tended to have mothers who were well educated and in a high socioeconomic class; babies who were less alert tended to have mothers from less supportive settings who had been more anxious during pregnancy. Further observation revealed a relationship between emotional stress during pregnancy and general restlessness in newborn infants. A. J. Ferreira, who has probably done the most work in this field, gave mothers, thirty-six weeks pregnant, an attitude questionnaire, and he later observed the behavior of their babies in the hospital nursery.[9] He found a correlation between the mother's emotions during pregnancy and the baby's behavior. Another study related a mother's anxiety in pregnancy to her newborn baby's crying: babies of highly anxious mothers cried more, particularly before feeding. The researchers felt that the differences must be due to prenatal or genetic factors rather than to differences in the mother's handling, because the variations in crying between babies of anxious and nonanxious mothers was more marked just before the mothers picked them up for feeding, and because the variations were found as early as the first four days of life. Sontag had already noticed a similar relationship back in 1941 when he looked at the infants of mothers who had experienced prolonged periods of severe anxiety during late pregnancy: these babies too were highly active and intolerant of delays in feeding.[10]

But it has become clear that babies are acutely sensitive to their surroundings and to the characteristics of their caregivers, even immediately after birth. Because of this, it is still an open question how much the baby's behavior is already influenced by the mother's handling even after only a day of being together. The only way of surely checking whether a baby's behavior stems from prenatal factors is to observe the baby before he has had any postnatal contact with the mother at all.

In some of the studies I have done of young infants, I feel I can pretty much tell in advance which babies will stay awake and not cry during the tests simply by talking to the mothers beforehand. This might be because the mother has in some way, pre- or postnatally, influenced the child's behavior, and I can recognize it from her anxiety; or it might be that she is making me so anxious that, when I handle the baby, I do it badly and the baby cries.

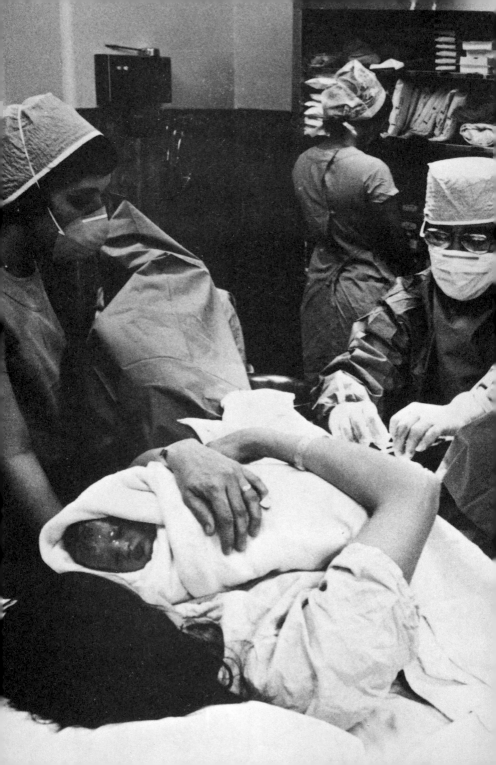

3 / The Delivery: When and Where

Two of the more contentious issues in modern obstetric practice are, first, the question of induction of labor: is it really necessary and, if so, when should it be done? Second, is a hospital the best place to have a baby or can some deliveries take place at home? The issues are difficult because they involve the questions of the role of the doctor in our society, the value attributed to scientific findings, and the way these findings are used.

Some of the problems arise from the fact that, thanks to contraception and abortion, we have a markedly decreasing birthrate and, thanks to better social conditions and better obstetrics, a decreasing deathrate for mothers and babies at the time of birth. A hundred years ago parents accepted the fact that many of their children would die at an early age. But now, along with considerable pressure for the number of offspring per family to be limited to two, there is widespread expectation that these children should live and be normal and healthy. It is only the present low deathrate at birth that allows us even to begin to consider the emotional quality of the experience and the long-term psychological consequences.

The new focus on these matters has resulted in an increasingly idealized insistence that pregnancy and delivery should not only be perfect as far as the physical health of mother and baby are concerned, but also that the experience should be perfect emotionally. Unfortunately these two attainments, given the current state of medicine, may not always be compatible. This does not mean that the ideal should not be sought, but the effort has to be tempered with the realization that perfection may not be possible.

It then comes to a question of values. Do we think that physiological perfection should be bought at the expense of possible psychological disadvantage, or are parents willing to take certain risks of physical damage in exchange for better emotional results? The situation is made all the more complicated by the fact that these decisions are made on behalf of the child as well, which puts vast responsibility on those concerned. We have to take into account what statistics are available. For instance, in medical research, relationships are often shown to exist between two factors. If a baby is in the uterus for more than forty-two weeks, there is an increased incidence of injury to him. This association may be definite but low: say five out of a hundred babies who prolong their stay in the uterus until forty-three weeks may suffer some kind of trouble. It may be impossible to determine which five babies out of the hundred will be the ones who suffer and which ninety-five will not. It is here that a value judgment is made. Do we induce a hundred babies to make sure that five will not suffer physical damage? And knowing that ninety-five babies will be induced without their needing it, are we exposing them in turn to the small risk of side-effects from the procedure?

In most cases the doctor is in the best position to know what the risks are, but it is also here that his role may be called into question. He can try and explain to the parents what the risks are, so that they can be involved in making an informed decision. Or he can act as an authority who thinks that he understands all the processes at work and is therefore justified in telling the parents what is going to happen and allowing them little role in the decision. In England the freedom of choice is slightly greater than in the United States. In many states in America, women are already bound by law to have their children in a hospital, attended by a doctor. In England, they still have the choice of home delivery, with a midwife, though in many areas this choice has become more theoretical than practical because domicilary services are being phased out.

INDUCTION

The mechanism by which labor gets underway is still a mystery, though this is not from lack of investigation but from the complexity of the processes involved. Normally at thirty-eight weeks after conception, give or take two weeks, uterine contractions will begin spontaneously. It is now thought that when the brain of the baby reaches a certain state of maturity, it releases a substance that begins a chain of reactions finally leading to delivery. It is obvious though, that a number of other factors are also involved.

It is possible to change this biological clock by medical induction. The methods commonly used are: first, artificially rupturing the membranous sac containing baby and amniotic fluid. This is done with surgical instruments, through the vagina and cervix, and sometimes also involves stripping the membranes away from the walls of the uterus. Second, administering a variety of drugs, either by mouth, by injection, or by intravenous drip. This last method is most popular because uterine contractions can be controlled by the rate at which the drug is administered into the vein. Third, introducing a drug directly into the uterus with a catheter. The drugs normally used are oxytocin, which has been available for a number of years and acts mainly by causing contractions, and the prostaglandins, which are becoming increasingly popular and act by causing both uterine contractions and cervical dilation. It is thought that none of these methods of induction bears much relationship to the mechanisms by which labor begins spontaneously.

Another relevant factor concerning induction is the state of the cervix. Before being delivered the baby obviously has to pass through the cervix, and it is now usual when induction is performed to assess the cervical condition by manual examination through the vagina. The cervix may be "ripe," when it is soft enough to allow easy passage of the baby, or it may still be hard and offer considerable resistance. Softening of the cervix normally occurs when the baby is near its full term in the uterus, as the result of hormones produced in the body. Although drugs may also affect softening, inductions done when the cervix is hard tend to be more painful and hazardous.

There are medical indications for inducing labor which are undoubtedly life-saving, and in these cases it is obvious that any detrimental emotional or behavioral effects will be of secondary importance. There is no question, when in certain cases induction is an absolute necessity, that this judgment rests largely with the doctor, who then has the responsibility of explaining the reasons to the parents. But the amount of disagreement that exists over such indications can be seen by looking at the rates at which women are induced in different obstetrical units. In some hospitals six to seven women out of every ten are induced, and there are obstetricians who advise all women to be induced; on the other hand, some units have induction rates of one or two out of ten. So there is a rate variation of at least between 10 percent and 70 percent in units dealing with similar mothers.

What are the advantages and disadvantages of induction? The absolute advantage is that in some cases it saves the mother or the child from death or damage. Some of the other more arguable advantages are that the mother is well rested; her stomach is empty because food can be restricted, which decreases danger if a general anesthetic has to be given; last-minute transport problems to a hospital are avoided; the mother is able to organize her life more efficiently if she knows when the delivery is going to occur.

There are philosophical as well as medical arguments against induction. The processes involved in birth have developed over millions of years; they are extremely complicated and our state of knowledge about them is still rudimentary. If one is going to interfere with such processes, one must not only be aware of the benefits but also continually investigate the side-effects, knowing that these may appear much later. Second, childbirth is an important emotional event in many people's lives (in Britain about 80 percent of the population become parents); if birth is to be controlled by specialists, using mechanical means, in large institutions, then it may sometimes adversely affect the development of confidence and the emotional development of the parents in their relationship with their child. No good long-term studies to judge these effects have been completed, though some are underway.

Of other possible disadvantages, several studies have shown that babies born to mothers who have been induced with oxytocin run a slightly higher risk of becoming jaundiced than babies born spontaneously. Heinz Prechtl, working in Holland, has shown that jaundice alters the behavior of the baby; while it lasts the baby tends to sleep more and to spend less time alert.[1]

Other studies have clearly indicated that mothers who have been induced need to have more pain-killing drugs than those who have not been. The effects of some of these drugs on the behavior of the baby are discussed later, but suffice it to say here that they do in some cases significantly alter the baby's behavior after birth.

There is also the question of separation of mother and baby immediately after birth. Studies indicate that the incidence of babies admitted to special-care units, away from their mothers, is considerably higher when birth is induced. Of course, these babies may have to go into special care not because of the induction but because of a reason that led to the induction in the first place. But a study done at Cambridge University, of a relatively small number of women and their babies, found little relation between medical or social reasons for induction and the rate at which the babies were admitted to special care.[2] The rate of admission of induced babies of both sorts was 34.4 percent, whereas the admission rate for noninduced babies was 17.4. In another study done in England, Sheila Kitzinger examined the reports sent in by mothers who attended the National Childbirth Trust classes.[3] Her results cannot be applied generally since this group of women might have been especially motivated toward natural childbirth, but she found that 24 percent of the induced babies had gone into special care as opposed to only 7 percent of the noninduced babies. There is no way of telling whether these admissions were related to the induction itself or to the reasons behind the inductions.

What about the subjective experiences of mothers? Not unexpectedly, the results are conflicting. In one study carried out by M. Ounstead, four groups of mothers were included: a group induced by intravenous oxytocin, a group induced by intravenous prostaglandins, a group induced by putting prostaglandins directly into the uterus, and a control group that was not induced. In all there were 235 mothers having first babies (and here again more babies from the induced group went to the special-care unit). On the day after delivery the women were asked whether labor and delivery were better, worse, or the same as anticipated. Of those giving a definite "better" or "worse" answer 78 percent of the induced group said the labor was better than expected, compared with 59 percent of the non-induced group. The answers about delivery revealed no difference between the groups. Followed up after four months, 76 of the original induced mothers were asked whether they would like to have an induction again: 24 percent said yes, 25 percent said they would not mind, and 51 percent said they did not want one again. These results have to be viewed against the fact that these mothers had no previous experience of childbirth as a basis for comparison.

In contrast to this, Kitzinger looked at the reports of 53 mothers who were induced and had delivered previous babies.[4] Of these, 30 percent said the induced labor was better than the previous labor; 64 percent thought it worse. The remaining 6 percent found it about the same. In a control group of noninduced mothers with previous babies, 96 percent said their labor was better than the previous labor. Now, as I have pointed out, the trouble with this study is that the women already had a moderately strong desire for natural delivery, and therefore it could be argued that their reports of their labors as worse than their previous ones should be taken not so much as a condemnation of induction itself as an expression of their failure to fulfill a desire for spontaneous delivery.

In the Cambridge study already mentioned, induced women having their first babies were asked about inductions before and after they delivered. The percentage who disliked induction increased from 45 before delivery to 74 after. For those who had delivered previous babies, the figures were 64.5 percent before and 69 percent after. There were several reasons given for not wanting inductions: the speed of labor prevents the body from acclimatizing itself, so that contractions are more painful; induction detracts from the birth experience because the speed makes the reality of the birth hard to accept; the quick succession of pains lead to panic, so that breathing control is lost; induction detracts from the excitement of labor; it leaves a feeling of having been somehow cheated.

In most of these studies, no attempt was made to differentiate between induction and speeded deliveries. Induction is, technically, simply the starting of labor; in speeded deliveries the drugs used to start labor are continued to keep the uterine contractions going.

HOME VERSUS HOSPITAL

In all discussions of home versus hospital delivery, the childbirth practices in the Netherlands inevitably come up. Holland has a lower deathrate among babies than either the United States or England, and yet a very substantial number of the deliveries are carried out at home.

G. J. Kloosterman, Professor of Obstetrics at the University of Amsterdam, has summarized the philosophy on which the organization of obstetrics in the Netherlands has been based since the beginning of this century.[5] "Childbirth in itself is a natural phenomenon and in the large majority of cases needs no interference whatsoever—only close observation, moral support, and protection against human meddling." A healthy woman who delivers spontaneously performs a job that cannot be improved upon. This job can be done in the best way if the woman is self-confident and stays in surroundings where she is the real center (as in her own home). It is possible during pregnancy, by thorough prenatal care, to divide expectant mothers into two groups: a large one that shows no recognizable symptoms of pathology (the so-called low-risk group) and a much smaller one in which there are signs of slight or even gross abnormalities. Only the high-risk group belongs in a good hospital under the care of specialists; the other is better off under the care of specialists in the physiology of childbirth, the midwife, or a general practitioner with special training in obstetrics.

In 1973, 196,974 babies were born in Holland, and of these approximately 99,000 were born at home. Great emphasis is put on the benefits of an organization called Maternity Home Help, whose purposes are to provide assistance during the delivery; to provide care for mother and child for eight to ten days after confinement; and to train home helpers to take the mother's place in the family during the lying-in period. In 1973, of the 99,000 home deliveries, 83,088 were attended by a home helper, midwives, or doctors with the cooperation of home helpers. The deathrate of the babies delivered at home was less than one third of the overall rate for the whole of the Netherlands, 4.5 per 1000 as against 16.3 per 1000 births.

The philosophy in Great Britain and the United States is quite different. It operates on the basis that it is impossible to predict which women will be "at risk," so that all women having babies must be treated as if they were high risks and hospitals are the places to deal with them. Therefore, if a mother has her baby at home, she is increasing the risks not only to her own health but to that of the baby. Again a question of values is involved. Each time a pregnant woman crosses a street she is increasing the risk of death for herself and her unborn baby, but no one would question her right to cross the street.

Is there any evidence that it makes a long-term difference if a baby is delivered at home or in the hospital? Hard scientific evidence is difficult to come by, and there probably never will be any definitive studies done because the associated issues are so many and so complex. There is some evidence that the incidence of depression after birth is increased in hospital deliveries. In one study the figures were that some depression occurred in 60 percent of hospital deliveries and in only 16 percent of home deliveries. It is also interesting to note that in a study of 601,222 spontaneous deliveries, there was a peak of births at 3:00 to 4:00 A.M., a time when the woman is likely to be in a quiet sheltered environment and in a sleepily peaceful emotional state; interestingly enough, the onset of labor also showed a peak at night.

With the reminder that one should always be very cautious about applying findings from studies of animals to human behavior, I want to review some of the evidence that environment affects labor in animals. Observation of animals in their natural habitat shows that many species seek out quiet and familiar surroundings in which to have their babies.[6] In one experiment, systematic work with artificial situations have been carried out with mice. Toward the end of pregnancy they were moved every half hour between a familiar nesting box and a glass bowl with rock bedding. Significantly more first births took place in the nesting box and, in general, significantly more pups were born in the familiar environment than in the glass bowl. In a further study, after the birth of their second pup in a litter, the mice were gently disturbed by a complete change of the smell and touch sensations of the environment. After this, the average labor time before the birth of the next pup in the litter was more than twenty minutes. In a similar but undisturbed group of mice used for comparison, it was only twelve or thirteen minutes. A third study involved three experimental groups of mice: toward the end of pregnancy, one group was given continuous disturbance, one periodic disturbance, and the third minimal disturbance. These environmental differences all influenced the time of arrival of the first pup, the timing of births in the later part of labor, and the number of pups who died in each group. Although comparable experiments with human beings have not been undertaken, for the obvious reasons, clinical observations of women during labor seem to indicate that environmental disturbances may affect the timing, strength, and efficiency of contractions.

Finally I would like to quote from a talk given by a pediatrician, John Davies, to a National Childbirth Trust seminar on home deliveries. He pointed out that there were positive and negative sides to every human activity: 'Nobody goes to sea only to sick . . . I feel very strongly myself that there is no point in a child being conceived, born and reared, unless birth has that positive side to it by which it is recognized as something adult human beings need and want to do in order to 'be themselves.' " There is no way to prove by statistics that a baby born at home is any better off than one born in hospital but:

> I do not think that the collection of figures to support a case is science. We are not dealing with matters that are susceptible to statistical analysis. I saw some of my children born at home and some born in excellent hospitals, and my personal experience squares with that of many women, that where you compare one experience that has gone well with another that has gone as well as it can, the quality of the experience at home is superior to that of the other. I cannot speak for the quality of the experience for the baby. Of course babies do not have memories that make them able to describe what was going on in the labour ward when they first opened their eyes. But there may be another, less systematized, kind of memory and it does not mean that the experience has been lost, or is not having an influence. Being received into a normal home where the mother is in command and at ease, and where the other children not only know but feel that the baby is a real addition to their family (and not brought back from Harrods, or whatever fantasy they may construct of the event), is likely to be the best way to enter life.

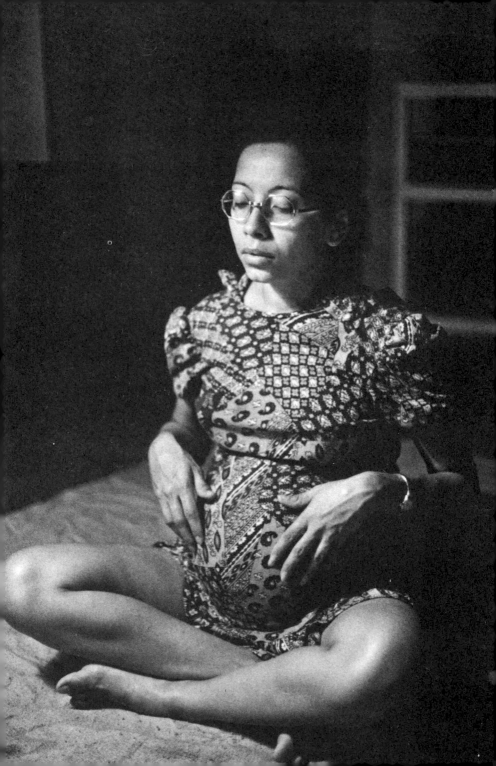

4 / Pain and Relief

Pain is a sensation that normally serves us well. If we get a splinter, pain encourages us to remove it before any damage occurs. In this context pain obviously has a survival value. But what about the pain of childbirth? Reproduction is vital to the survival of any species and it seems strange that, in humans and higher animals, birth is so often associated with extreme pain, for this might be thought to have a discouraging effect. That it doesn't may be a tribute to the pleasures of sex or the shortness of people's memory about pain in childbirth. But why, considering the usual course of natural selection, should birth be associated with pain? Why is it there? And does it perform any function?

It was a popular theory thirty years ago that the pains of childbirth were a feature of modern society and that women in primitive cultures did not feel them. The idea gained ground that, if we could become "natural" again, our society too could return to a state where childbirth was pain-free. But observation of people still living in primitive societies around the world appears to show that there is no culture in which childbirth is painless, and in many cultures women have a much worse time than in our own. As Margaret Mead puts it, "Childbirth may be experienced according to the phrasing given it by the culture, as an experience that is dangerous and painful, interesting and engrossing, matter of fact and mildly hazardous, or accompanied by enormous supernatural hazards."[1]

Anatomically it should have been possible for us to develop as a species without nerves that send pain sensations from the uterus, vagina, or perineum. The last two are exquisitely sensitive to pleasure sensations, and it may be that pain fibers (which are separate from nerves carrying pleasure sensations) are necessary in these areas in order to protect them from damage. If this is so, then they are going to be hugely stimulated by the infant's head passing through what is normally a relatively narrow canal.

What of animals? Do they suffer during childbirth and, if so, what effect does it have? Eugene Marais, in *The Soul of the Ape*,[2] makes a point that has also been noted by others: in lower animals the process of reproduction is as simple as it is painless; it is only in higher animals, with their greatly reduced birthrates, that we meet the first indications of birth pain; and as a sure and proportionate accompaniment, we find a need for maternal care of the immature young. Experiments with animals that do experience pain in childbirth show that in certain species, drugs given to remove pain alter behavior toward the young after birth. Marais observed a herd of buck in which, for fifteen years, there had been no case of a mother's refusing to look after her young under normal conditions. He took ten of the animals and made them either totally or partially unconscious with drugs during delivery, allowing them to recover shortly afterwards. In all cases these animals rejected their newborns and refused to mother them. He took another group of animals and made them unconscious just after birth for about thirty minutes; these animals did not reject their newborns. It would be very dangerous to draw any definite conclusions from these findings about how humans behave or, for that matter, how other animals behave. For instance, a goat made unconscious just after delivery and then given its newborn would undoubtedly reject it; in this species the period just after birth is vital for the development of nurturing. It is possible, however, to put forward the theory that pain, along with many other processes, does play some part in the development of a mother's feelings for her baby.

Another theory of the use of pain is that it may serve in some way to help keep mothers alert during labor and in the period immediately after delivery. Many mothers and babies who have gone through a normal labor and delivery without drugs also experience an hour or two of extreme alertness following delivery. In terms of muscle usage labor is fantastically exhausting, and it may be that pain counteracts the sensations of fatigue.

This could be mediated by hormones, for Russian researchers have found that the secretion of adrenaline appears to be related to feelings of pain.

In humans, there are at least two contributing factors to the sensation of pain. First there is the nerve message to the brain following stimulation or damage to some area of the body. Second there is the state of the brain when it receives the message, and this is affected by cultural expectations about pain, previous experience of it, anxiety, fear, fatigue, and expectations about the outcome of the pain. If you hit your finger with a hammer, pain predicts a bruised finger. In labor, pain predicts the birth of a baby.

People differ greatly in their anatomy and physiology, so there are individual differences in the number of pain messages reaching the brain. Thus some women have totally painless births, no matter what conditions prevail. These are commonly said to total between 7 and 14 percent of all women, though I personally find that figure very high and suspect that 3 or 4 percent would be more accurate. But there is still a great deal of debate about how, when pain messages reach the brain, they are altered by psychological factors. It is hard to measure pain in an objective way. Researchers have attempted to measure pain by looking at associated changes in body functions, such as dilation of the pupil, speed up of the pulse, changes in blood flow through the skin, and changes in blood pressure. These have proved unreliable. In any case, objective measurement may not be very helpful if what matters is how pain is perceived.

Some people have tried to use certain kinds of behavior, such as grimacing, grinding the teeth, frequent crying out, or tears, as indicators of the severity of pain; but behavior is almost totally dependent on cultural expectations about what people do in pain. It is, after all, fairly frequent in our society that an obstetrician delivers a woman in what he thinks is an ideal, uncomplicated, and straightforward way, only to learn that she has found the whole thing utterly harrowing. The reverse is also true. (Unfortunately this sometimes leads a doctor to disbelieve a mother, or at least to feel she is exaggerating, on the grounds that her observations do not coincide with his own. But there is no reason why they should, for the birth is being seen from two very different vantages, and expectations of acceptable behavior need in no way coincide.) Recently researchers in Wales did an experiment where women in labor were asked to squeeze an object during each contraction according to how much pain they were having. The object they squeezed was attached to a recording machine that measured how much pressure the woman was exerting. What they discovered was that, very early on in labor, the women were already squeezing as hard as they possibly could and therefore were unable to squeeze any harder later, even if the pain grew worse.

The psychological aspects of pain have been demonstrated in various other ways. For instance, if people being tested for the maximum level of pain they can stand are given an injection of sterile water which they are told is a pain killer, they will in many cases report an increased tolerance to pain even though the water itself could not have helped.[3] This is the so-called placebo effect.

For the last twenty years researchers in the Soviet Union have been studying the effects of psychoprophylaxis (psychological and physical preparation by instruction and practice) and hypnosis on the pain of childbirth. These methods induce relaxation during birth in order to prevent the muscles of the pelvis from tensing up and thus making the uterine contractions less effective and the pressure against the pelvic tissues greater. The methods thus decrease the amount of pain messages going to the brain, and they might also alter the woman's perceptions or her ability to control such messages when they did get to the brain. The overall finding from the Soviet research, which has been based on observations of many thousands of mothers during delivery, is that psychoprophylaxis and hypnosis both decrease not only the pain of childbirth but also the incidence of birth complications. In many of their studies the Russians have used a five-point scale to judge the amount of pain: (5) maximum success, no pain, the mother conscious and active throughout the labor, (4) complaints of short duration with endurable pain, (3) failure in spite of some temporary pain relief, (2) and (1) complete failure. In one study of five hundred women, comparing psychoprophylaxis with drugs, the failure rate (that is, women in groups 3, 2, and 1) was 47 percent with drugs—this was before the days of epidural anesthesia—and 33 percent with psychoprophylaxis.[4]

Another recent and unpublished study done by C. Fisher in England examines pain-killing drugs given during labor when antenatal care, delivery, and early mother-child care after delivery were all handled by a single person—a midwife—with deliveries either done at home or in the general-practitioner unit attached to the local maternity hospital. One hundred consecutive births were analyzed: of the 55 women having their first baby 21 (38 percent) needed no drugs, and of the 45 having their second, third, or fourth babies, 38 (84 percent) needed no drugs. The comparable figures for the maternity unit of the same hospital show a very much higher usage of pain-killing drugs.

METHODS OF RELIEF

Be they chemical, psychological, or magical, attempts to relieve the pain of childbirth are probably as old as humanity. In our own culture, the methods used include drugs, psychoprophylaxis, hypnosis, and acupuncture.

Drugs. Drugs to help with birth pain were first used in England in 1847 by James Young Simpson, who used ether. Six years later Queen Victoria gave birth to Prince Leopold under chloroform administered by John Snow, and she was said to show approval. Since then a huge variety of chemical substances have been inhaled, swallowed, and injected into various parts of the body in an effort to deal effectively with pain in labor and delivery.

The method now employed with most frequent success in both England and the United States is epidural anesthesia. A local anesthetic is introduced into the space around the spinal cord with a needle or tube; the drug blocks the transmission of messages along the nerves carrying sensation from the legs and abdomen. This anesthetic does not appear to interfere with uterine contractions, though the mechanisms by which the baby is actually delivered may not be as efficient (several studies of epidural deliveries indicate an increased need for the use of forceps). Its other advantage is that it has little effect on the level of consciousness of the mother; she can be aware of the course of delivery even if, because of the loss of sensation, less able to participate actively. The method is in most cases both effective and safe. The drugs, however, do enter the mother's bloodstream and via the placenta enter the baby's blood too; one recent study indicates that for a period after birth some of these babies may have decreased muscle strength and tone.[5]

Pethidine (meperidine, demerol) has for the last ten years, before the advent of epidurals, held prime place among drugs. It is frequently used in combination with another drug, levallorphan, which counteracts the effects that pethidine has on breathing. How exactly pethidine works is difficult to assess, for it is a morphia derivative and causes very definite changes in consciousness and in the way the outside world is perceived. Many mothers describe the sensation as "feeling drunk," "being out of control," "feeling very drowsy and distant." Whether it acts by altering the perception of pain once the messages have reached the brain, or whether it actually decreases the messages reaching the brain, is difficult to tell. A study done at one London hospital attempted to assess how good a pain killer pethidine was.[6] Three groups of pregnant women were given a test to see what their pain threshold was. Pressure was applied to the skin covering the bone in the front of the lower leg. The groups were then either given an injection of sterile water, pethidine alone, or pethidine and levallorphan, and then tested again at varying intervals to see if their pain threshold had changed. In all three groups the threshold remained virtually the same, with only minor variations, and the peculiar conclusion of the study was that pressure on the lower leg was not a suitable way of judging the effects of drugs on labor pains. But other studies have indicated that pethidine does have a pain-killing effect, and this surely must be so or its use would have never continued at the rate it has.

The effects of drugs on both mother and baby have always been extremely carefully monitored by the medical profession and others, and the importance of this was emphasized in the 1960s when it was discovered that barbiturates given to mothers during labor tended to depress respiration in babies. They were abandoned, but previously, while they were still in use, the pediatrician Berry Brazelton found that babies born to mothers who had had barbiturates were reported to be poor at sucking and difficult to feed.[7] He also discovered that they were slower in gaining weight than babies born to mothers without drugs.

Other work has shown that babies born under barbiturates sucked slower, with less pressure, and took less at each feeding. At about the same time, Gerald Stechler was doing some research on perception that involved finding out what babies aged two to four days liked to look at.[8] He presented them with three cards; on one was printed the outline of a face, on the second three dots, and on the third nothing. They looked most at the one with the face, less at the three dots, and least at the blank card. Although this is interesting in itself, what is significant here is that babies born to mothers under barbiturates (and also under pethidine) looked at the cards less than those babies born to mothers without drugs. This is perhaps not very surprising since the drugs alter one's state of consciousness, and when they are injected they rapidly cross over the placenta to the baby. Drugs do stay in babies longer than in adults because babies are less equipped to get rid of them in the usual way, by breaking them down into other substances and then peeing them out. But why effects should last for several days and even longer is still the subject of much speculation.

These findings greatly intrigued psychologists, who followed them up with their own observations of babies. Yvonne Brackbill specifically looked at the effect of pethidine on babies.[9] She had examined, first, its effect on what some people regard as the most primitive form of learning in babies: habituation, by which a baby (or anyone else) comes to take no notice of some stimulation he initially found disturbing. Brackbill played a relatively loud sound to babies in short bursts over and over again, to see how long they would take to stop reacting to it. Babies born to the pethidine mothers took over twice as long to stop reacting to the noise as those babies born to non-pethidine mothers. In another study they tended to be less responsive in turning toward the sound of a voice, were less cuddly, and less consolable when they cried. Martin Richards and Judy Dunn found that babies born under the pethidine and levallorphan mixture showed altered sucking behavior.[10] If a baby showed differences in behavior, they thought, this might affect his mother's way of responding to him. They observed the mothers feeding their babies and found that indeed the pethidine mothers had to stimulate their babies more during each feeding and that the feedings were shorter and more often interrupted. It is not yet clear what the longer-term significance of this might be. I have myself over the last few years made a large number of observations on babies to see how much they can see, hear, and smell, and what kinds of things they like to see, hear, and smell. In every case I have looked to see whether the drug used during delivery had an effect, and in only one so far have I found this to be so: in my study of whether babies can tell where a voice is coming from, babies of pethidine mothers generally performed less well.[11]

To turn quickly to other well-known methods of relief: Inhalants, such as nitrous oxide, which have now been used for some time, seem to alter the consciousness of the mother for a short period and so far have not been shown to have a significant effect on the behavior of the baby. With general anesthesia, when the mother is made completely unconscious, the drugs do cross the placenta and will affect some of the baby's functions, but little research has been done on this so far. What has been done indicates that the babies are affected by the anesthetic agents for a period of time after birth.

With the knowledge now available, new drugs are going through much more exhaustive testing, but it is of course only too likely that chemical substances introduced into the body will have effects other than the desired one. In light of our assessment of the need for drugs in childbirth, it is extremely interesting to compare the rate of use in different countries. According to recent surveys, drugs are given for pain in only 5 percent of deliveries in Holland and in 12 percent of deliveries in Sweden. Equivalent drugs are given in more than 80 percent of deliveries in England. English women are not particularly noted to be any less stoical than their European counterparts—but why is there this huge difference? Is it because English doctors and midwives feel that drugs should be given routinely? Or could it be that Dutch and Swedish women know childbirth is going to be painful but accept pain as part of the whole process, whereas English women have been conditioned to believe that pain must be relieved?

Psychoprophylaxis. We have already met this method in the context of Soviet research. Its aim is to teach women the processes, both physical and mental, that occur during pregnancy, labor, delivery, and the early moments of the baby's life, so that they will feel able to control and help their own bodies' actions. It is an essentially active venture: the mother controls the labor and delivers her child, with others there to assist when asked.

Quite independently of the work in the USSR, in 1933 Grantly Dick-Read published *Childbirth Without Fear* to show how women could aid childbirth by learning how to relax.[12] Fear and anxiety, he proposed, cause tension, and tension causes pain. In the 1940s Fernand Lamaze, a French obstetrician working in a Communist trade-union clinic in Paris, traveled to Russia and brought back the idea that women who had been properly instructed in pregnancy could actively control their labor delivery. His assumption was that childbirth is an essentially psychosomatic process and that both psychological and physical preparation are essential. Since then, within the "natural childbirth" movement, the emphasis put on the mind or on the body has varied, from country to country and from one time to another.

In the simplest of terms, current methods used to teach natural childbirth endeavor to instill confidence in the mother by instructing her, and generally her husband too, in the actual physiological processes of pregnancy and birth. A series of classes are taught to give her an understanding and control of the changes occurring in her body. The groups are usually headed by a trained instructor, and an important part of the instruction is hearing the experience of others. The methods include practice of special breathing exercises, which are keyed to the uterine contractions typical of the different stages of labor.

The pain-reducing procedures generally taught throughout the world are techniques that aid the mother in maintaining control; and techniques that can be practiced during confinement to relax the muscles and collaborate actively with the expulsive efforts. The studies made in the USSR strongly support the idea that such preparation both reduces pain and improves obstetrics. In Great Britain and the United States, however, it has been found that such studies are very difficult to assess. The main argument against their reliability is that a certain kind of woman (usually middle-class in our culture) is disposed toward psychoprophylaxis, perhaps because of education, greater leisure, and so on, and that any differences found between those using this method for dealing with pain and those using other methods may be due to the personalities of the women rather than to the method itself. Ideally, to get around this, a study would have to be arranged in which mothers were randomly assigned to have psychoprophylaxis or some other method of pain killing, but quite rightly that would be unacceptable on ethical grounds. However, studies done in many Western countries indicate that women who have had psychoprophylactic training do in fact get fewer drugs. I use the word "get" deliberately because, for them, getting fewer drugs is probably dependent on several factors. For instance, they may actually feel less pain, or they may feel that it would be a waste of their training if they allowed themselves to be given drugs, or it may just be that they are better able to refuse drugs in cases where they are routinely administered. Since the husband is included in the instruction, he can support his wife in all these matters.

At present the main development in psychoprophylaxis is toward better emotional and psychological preparation. For example, Sheila Kitzinger's book *The Experience of Childbirth* integrates birth into the whole course of a woman's sexual development. Her method might therefore be called "psychosexual."[13]

Hypnosis and acupuncture. Hypnosis is a reversible mental state, produced in one person by another, that involves an increased susceptibility to suggestion which can lead to sensory and physical changes. Methods of using hypnosis in childbirth vary: some use posthypnotic suggestion, others have delivered the child while the mother is actually hypnotized. Many argue about whether the pain of childbirth is actually reduced by this method or whether it simply produces a memory block against recalling the pain; but hypnosis does not in fact automatically block the memory of events, so there may be a real reduction. Again, Russian researchers have claimed that the method is effective, although a recent study of a very large number of consecutive deliveries in women who had been given hypnotic conditioning found that only 7 percent of them had painless births—a figure, you will remember, comparable to that claimed for unprepared women. Leon Chertok, in his book on psychosomatic methods, thinks that hypnosis, suggestion, and psychoprophylaxis operate by similar means in affecting the experience of pain in labor.[14] He regards "suggestion" as the common factor in all these techniques, though feels that other effects may also be involved.

Recently there has been a resurgence of interest in acupuncture as a means of relieving birth pain, but it has been noted that, although Chinese textbooks on the subject indicate that acupuncture can be used for the treatment of such obstetric complications as a prolonged second stage of labor, there is relatively little written about relieving pain. One reason for this might be that, although acupuncture has been used in China for a thousand years therapeutically, its use for operative pain killing is fairly recent.

Moxacombustion, the burning of some kind of moxa (usually *Artemesia vulgaris*) at an acupuncture site, is the discipline's recommendèd method for the relief of childbirth pain. Though few deliveries are now being done in the West using these methods, they are becoming more popular. One report on fifteen cases claimed complete success in six cases and six complete failures; but these last women, it was thought, were either too fat or too frightened. Nonetheless, there are some who are confident that acupuncture will play an important role in pain relief during childbirth.

TRANSCRIPT: MRS. A, AGED 25, FIRST BABY (A GIRL)

Father	Mother	Midwife
		Oops, oops. Show her. It's a little girl—welcome darling.
Wow, there she is! Didn't take very long to come out, did you?	Oh lovely, oh lovely. Oh, a cough.	
	Oh, that was nice.	Very nice.
	Oh, that was very nice. A hiccough. That was the sherry last night.	
Ah, oh, was it?		There, look.
(laughs)	Hello.	
	Oh dear, what a lot of noise.	Well, if that was the sherry, you must have had a lot of sherry last night.
Yes.	Oh.	
		Two little bits under the arms there.

No vernix.

What a funny-coloured beast.

    Oh, how nice.

What a big one, isn't it?

    It's not a funny colour. It's very nice.

I'm very satisfied.

    (laughs) Are you satisfied?

    Oh dear—just floods all over the place. Just try to keep out of it for a moment.

(baby given to mother)

    Oh, hello. Hello. Oh, you're nice. That's a lot of noise for a little girl. That's right—you've opened your eyes. That's lovely.

Oh well, that's a nice normal beast, isn't it. Hello.

    Oh, that's good, that's very good. That's a very good and nice noise.

Miaow.

    No, not miaow, that's the other sort.

That's nice.

Father	Mother	Midwife
	Oh you're nice. What a nice beast. Oh, a hiccough. Oh, a hiccough.	
Aah! Well done—it was clever of you. It only took six hours and ten minutes. That's very clever.		
		Has she got a name, actually?
	Oh.	
	To be known as Kirsty, we hope.	
Christina Margaret.		
		How nice.
	Hello. Do you like it? Well, don't squeeze your face up like that. What a silly thing to do. We'll call you Albert if you're not careful.	
Aah, miaow.		
	Ow!	
She's got nice skin.		
	Very nice skin—pretty colour too.	
Mmm—virginal white.		
	Oh.	

Oh, not very nice though, is it?

Not yet. Yes, you have lovely lungs.

Mmm. Hasn't opened its eyes. What colour are its eyes?

I don't know what colour.

Got the shakes?

I had the shakes all the time since last night.

Absolutely babylike too. Born to all these strange-shaped heads and things. You are perfectly normal.

Oh, you are a beautiful baby.

Oh, oh. You're not a Cameron at all.

There's not another one inside, is there?

There isn't, no. A hiccough.

Do you want me to go and make the phone call?

Yes. Sorry—that was the noise I was making because I was being sick.

Father	Mother	Midwife
She's a very good-looking child. What colour are your eyes? Blue, she says. Aah, waah (*imitates baby crying*).		
	We were determined. We had avocado pear with rather nice mustardy sauce, and the wienerschnitzel and broccoli and sauté potatoes, followed by chocolate charlotte.	
		That will teach you. Serve you right when you are beginning to go into labour.
	I didn't really think. I thought I was due Wednesday so I noshed up whilst I could.	
		Yes!
	I'm sorry I'm shaking, little beasty.	
	You're a big beasty, mind you. Oh (*imitates baby*). Oh (*imitates baby*). What a shame, what a shame.	Fancy calling your daughter a little beasty!

That was water and an unusual amount of it.

It's rather a mess, isn't it. She's got fabulous eyelashes.

She looks like her grandmother.

See how her colour is changing.

It's nice—got my nose and my ears. Not at all yours.

Rubbish. Oh!

Well, I think we'll have to tell Charity you've had a girl.

Do you fancy a green apple? I brought you one 'cause you said you wanted one.

I'm sorry, I can't pull it out because I shall cause a tidal wave (to baby). Oh, that's a nice tongue.

Oh, I probably shan't.

Bend your legs up, love.

I'm sorry about my legs shaking.

That's all right—you can't help it.

It's a bit hard with the sheet there.

OK.

Push. Come on, bit harder.

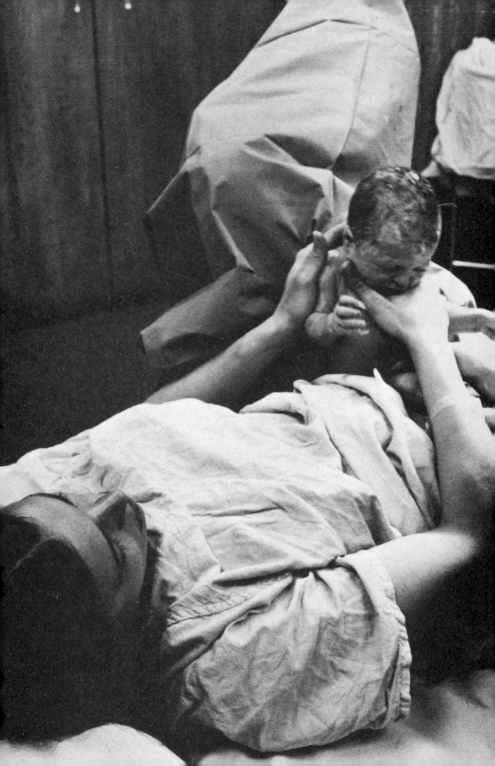

5 / The First Minutes

After the long months of watching and feeling an abdomen slowly enlarging, of being aware of the changing movements of the fetus, of experiencing labor and delivery—which has been likened to climbing to the top of a very high mountain—what then of that first moment after birth when parents and baby meet one another face to face? What are the mother's feelings when she first actually sees the child of her own flesh and blood, the child she already knows so intimately and for whom she will be responsible for at least the next fifteen years?

The normal routine in hospitals after the baby is born varies considerably, but in general the cord is cut and tied, the baby's mouth and throat are cleared of any fluid, and the baby is wrapped up and observed for a short period to ensure that regular breathing has been established and that he is a good color. Upon birth, it is common for whoever is handling the baby to record his heartrate, muscle tone, and breathing and color. This "Apgar score" serves as a permanent record of the baby's condition and can be used for reference later if necessary. Then, still well wrapped up (heat loss from the skin of the baby is so rapid that his temperature can drop very fast), the baby is handed to the mother.

In this book I have included transcripts of a series of deliveries recorded on videotape as part of a research project I was doing to find out how mothers and babies got to know one another's needs over the first few months after birth. I talked to the mothers when they were about thirty-six weeks' pregnant with their first baby. At that time I asked them what they expected labor and delivery to be like, as well as how they thought they would care for the baby later: I was interested to see how actually having a baby would change these ideas. All the mothers had uncomplicated pregnancies and volunteered to take part.

In looking at the mother's and baby's behavior in the delivery room, I was following up some marvelous work done in the United States by pediatricians Marshall Klaus and John Kennell.[1] They had filmed twelve mothers with their full-term infants some time between thirty minutes and thirteen hours after birth. In order to allow the mother maximum freedom in handling her baby, both mother and baby were put under a radiant heater so that the baby could be naked with no fear of his getting cold: their films lasted ten minutes each and covered the mother's first contact with her baby (except for the brief look at him immediately after delivery). From these films Klaus and Kennell made records of each child's movements, the position of his mother's fingertips and palms on his body, head, hands, and feet; the amount of time the mother spent smiling; the amount of time she spent either physically supporting or cradling him with her hands; and the amount of time the two of them spent *en face* (that is, with heads aligned so that they could look into one another's eyes).

The results of these observations showed that each mother went through an "orderly and predictable" pattern of behavior when she first examined her newborn infant. Beginning hesitantly with her fingertips, she touched his hands and feet and then within four or five minutes began to caress his body with the palms of her hands, showing increasing excitement as she did so. This examination continued for several minutes, and then diminished as the mother dozed off with the naked baby at her side. During the ten minutes of filming there was also a marked increase in the time that the mother positioned herself and her baby so that they could look into one another's eyes (if the baby had his eyes open). At the same time, she showed intense interest in waking her infant in an attempt to get him to open his eyes, and this was verbalized by nearly three quarters of the mothers: "Open your eyes, oh come on now, open your eyes," or "If you open your eyes I'll know you're alive." Several mothers also mentioned that, once the infant looked at them, they felt much closer to him.

Klaus and Kennell reviewed studies done on the behavior of

animals immediately after giving birth, and they think that the reactions described above are specific to human beings. They also speculate that, just as in the rhesus monkey, there are clear-cut patterns and orders of behavior—cradling, grooming, nursing, restraining, retrieving—that are components in establishing early affectional ties between animal mothers and their newborn offspring, so may this period immediately after birth also be especially sensitive for the development of affectional ties in human beings too.

My own observations of mothers and their babies differ in many ways from Klaus's and Kennell's because I was looking at the time in the delivery room immediately after birth, starting from the time the baby's head was delivered, through to his being given to his mother, sometimes to his father, and to the time he was taken away to be washed and weighed. In this situation the baby was well wrapped up, and the only exposed parts were the head and sometimes small pink hands and feet.

I recorded twelve deliveries, all of them in similar delivery rooms in a large maternity hospital. Some of them were in the consultant unit and attended by obstetricians, and some of them were in the general-practitioner unit in the same hospital. In the latter cases the delivery was performed by a midwife, usually well known to the mother, with the mother's practitioner standing by. In general it was a relatively short time between the delivery and the time the baby was given to the mother to hold: between 1 minute 25 seconds and 9 minutes, with an average for the group of about 3.5 minutes. This delay was the period in which the mouth was cleared and the baby was observed to make sure his breathing was all right. The baby was with the mother for an average of 6.5 minutes, but it varied between 1 minute and 15.5 minutes. When holding their babies, the mothers spent nearly three quarters of the time looking at them, and a third of that time smiling or laughing. Nine of the twelve mothers talked directly to their babies, and on an average all mothers spent about 80 percent of the time with both hands supporting or holding the baby, though again the variation was large—0 to 100 percent, in fact.

This is all rather dry information and conveys nothing of the emotional complexity, richness, and passion of what actually happens. Looking at and listening to my videotapes of deliveries, certain marked differences as well as similarities showed up between the Klaus and Kennell study and my own. Although many of the mothers did start by touching the babies with their fingertips, few progressed to stroking with the palms of the hands and few manipulated the hands and feet. This progression was hampered in most cases because the baby was wrapped up, and there were also differences resulting from the procedures for delivering the placenta and from alterations in position and interruptions as episiotomies were sewn up.

But there were many other factors influencing behavior. There was, most obviously, the mother's individual personality and the way she reacted to the situation, unique in all aspects. There was the factor of what drugs she had been given to relieve pain; a drug like pethidine would interfere with her normal perception of the world. In other cases it was an epidural, which removed all sensation from the lower half of her body. Then, too, sometimes the father was present, sometimes not. Sometimes the mother might have seen the midwife throughout pregnancy and had the chance of forming a relaxed and trusting relationship; in other cases the mother was delivered by an obstetrician and nurses who were completely unknown, on duty for that particular day in the hospital. The expression of deep emotions within our society very much depends on social custom. Childbirth is perhaps the one time when it is always acceptable to show emotions, but this still strongly depends on who is present to see and hear them. If the father is there, or others who are well known, it is far more likely that the mother will openly demonstrate her feelings, be they joy, despondency, or anything else. The length of labor, the difficulty of the delivery, the sex of the child, and much more, all seem to play their part in influencing behavior in these first minutes.

What I find particularly fascinating is what the mothers say. Obviously the situation is in some ways beyond the bounds of convention, and there is no correct or incorrect thing to say or way to behave. Along with Klaus and Kennell, I noted the intense interest in the baby's eyes. Of course, the baby's eyes needed to be open, and with my deliveries this happened with only three of the twelve. Mrs. C in the transcript here does not actually greet the baby directly until he opens his eyes, and then says "Hello!" to him seven times in less than one and a half minutes. Just prior to this she has asked her baby to open his eyes.

There is also the parents' adjustment to the sex of their child, especially where they had strongly desired a child of the opposite sex. In Mrs. D's delivery the baby is held up for the father to see, who says "It's a boy" though in fact it's a girl. The midwife and the mother correct him, and he admits "I got my things sorted out wrong." They all then exchange bantering remarks about the fact that she won't be able to play rugby. I think that behind this banter there is a very serious grappling with the baby's being a girl, an adjustment that starts at this moment and probably takes a considerable time to complete.

In some of the transcripts the mother verbalizes her detailed initial examination of the child. Mrs. C goes over the baby, touching here and there with her fingers and remarking to her husband, "Look at his little mouth—Look at his little face—His little nails—His little squashed-up nose, like your nose—Look at his little head—Look at his hair." A sort of joyous, wondering inventory and, at the same time, a serious check to make sure that everything is there as it is meant to be.

Another fairly common thing among new mothers, which I have noted not only from this particular study but also from other deliveries I have watched, is for them to note how some feature of the baby's anatomy is just like the father's. Mrs. B says, "She's got your little tiny nose," and Mrs. C, "His little squashed-up nose, like your nose." In the case of Mrs. A it is the husband who likens the baby to himself, "It's nice, got my nose and my eyes." Although I would agree that frequently a combination of the baby's features may look like one parent's or the other's, it seems odd to point out any particular feature. The nose seems especially common, which again to me is strange since a baby's nose is actually very different from an adult's nose. It is usually the mother who likens the child to the father rather than the other way round, and I cannot help speculating whether this is the mother saying to the father, "Look, this really is *your* baby because it looks like you." After all, they both know it is her baby—she has just given birth.

A mother's first response to her baby is by no means always positive, and Kenneth Robson and Howard Moss, in a study of fifty-four women having their first babies, found that most women described some initial feelings of strangeness, distance, and unfamiliarity toward their offspring, which persisted for at least the first few weeks of life.[2] Henry Kempe and his associates did a study that involved filming a very large number of mothers, in hospital delivery rooms, to see whether it was possible to predict from the mother's greeting her later relationship with the baby.[3] Some of the mothers showed distinct distaste and disgust as the baby was presented to them, and by scoring certain aspects of maternal behavior at this time Kempe did find that he could tell whether the mother would have a hard time forming normal relationships with her child later.

THE BABY'S EXPERIENCE

Most of us have no memory of our own births but, as John Davies said, this "does not mean that the experience is lost or is not having any influence." There are those who have reexperienced their birth by the use of drugs or hypnosis, and many have found the experience to be unpleasant, even traumatic. There are other ways for us to try and estimate what the experience is for the baby. We can as adults imagine what it's like to be squeezed through a narrow tube, which is warm, dark, wet, and only slightly yielding, for several hours. We can also observe the baby, during or just after birth, to see whether the experience he has just undergone seemed traumatic. There is the possibility that during delivery itself the baby is only semiconscious. Before birth the fetus is sensitive to touch: when a needle is put into the amniotic fluid (through the mother's abdominal and uterine wall, using local anesthetic) and touches the baby itself, the baby tries to move the touched part away from the needle. This may well be a reflex, and the baby may not be conscious of either the needle or the movement. Observations make it clear, though, that a baby can feel pain immediately after delivery and, unless one proposes some very delicate switch to turn on sensitivity to pain only after birth, it seems reasonable to assume that the infant is also capable of feeling pain during birth.

Immediately after a spontaneous delivery, where the mother has received no drugs and there were no other complications, the baby is often remarkably alert. After the first unique cry, expanding the lungs that have till now been filled with fluid, the child will, if kept warm and handled gently, lie quietly with his eyes open and looking around. If you move your face very slowly backward and forward about nine inches away from his, he may follow you with jerky, uncoordinated eye movements. Another reported observation is that if a clicking noise is made close to one ear and then to the other, he will tend to turn his eyes toward the click.[4] So probably the baby not only can see and hear but can also make attempts to determine which of two sides a sound is coming from and to keep a stimulating sight within the field of vision.

The French obstetrician Frederick Leboyer, from his extensive experience of watching childbirth, feels in no uncertain terms that the processes of birth are agony for the child: "Hell exists, and is white hot. It is not a fable. But we go through it at the beginning of our lives, not the end. Hell is what the child goes through to reach us. Its flames assail the child from every side; they burn its eyes, its skin, they sear its flesh; they devour. This fire is what the baby feels as the air rushes into the lungs. The air, which enters and sweeps through the trachea, and expands the alveoli, is like acid poured on a wound."[5] A powerful description. For my part, after watching babies very closely after delivery, I am surprised at how untraumatized they seem to be. Frequently after the first loud cry, the baby quiets down rapidly and lies still, apparently content to try and come to terms with his new surroundings. There is no way of actually knowing, of course—we can only surmise.

Leboyer, quite correctly, points out that we know the newborn infant can see, hear, and is exquisitely sensitive to his surroundings. The baby should therefore be treated and respected as a real person, who is having to make a very rapid adaptation from the only familiar environment he has known—the semidark, rhythmically noisy, water-suspended, warm and pulsating squeezing world of the uterus—to a sudden blast of noise, light, cold, and air. During this same period the baby's method of getting oxygen completely changes; instead of being transmitted from the blood of the mother across the placenta to the baby's blood, it has to come from the baby's own lungs, and this involves huge changes in the circulation of blood through his body.

To help the baby make these changes a little less rapidly, giving him more time to adapt, Leboyer suggests that, after the head has been delivered, the lights in the room should be dimmed and everyone should remain silent or at least talk in whispers. Then, when the rest of the delivery has taken place, and before the cord is cut, the baby should be placed immediately on the mother's tummy so that he can again feel direct contact with her. This will also help to keep the baby warm and perhaps, with one ear against the abdominal wall, reassured by hearing the rhythmical thud of the maternal heartbeat. At this stage, Leboyer feels, everyone must learn to wait. The cord should not be cut immediately but should be allowed to undergo the normal physiological changes that close off the blood supply from the placenta as the baby makes his first attempts at breathing. During this time he encourages the mother to massage her baby, to get to know what he feels like and to allow him gradually to become aware of what she feels like, externally. Later the doctor immerses the child in warm water, returning him to the weightlessness of the uterus.

Leboyer does not make scientific claims but simply says "Look and see for yourself." If his ideas become widely adopted, it will not be because of their scientific rightness or wrongness, but because our society wants to accept them at this particular moment in time. I think that Leboyer will be accepted, even though I also think that delivering a baby into complete silence when he has been surrounded by rhythmical sound might be terrifying. In fact, when the child is born, he still has fluid in the middle ear, which dampens noises until the fluid is absorbed over the first week. As a pediatrician I also wonder about the dangers of putting the child into water immediately after birth. The baby's ability to control his temperature is exceedingly poor at this stage, and keeping babies warm has been one of the real advances in reducing infant deaths in this period after birth. Still, none of these things should detract from the basic premise that the child is born a sensitive human being and needs to be treated as such.

THE FATHER'S PRESENCE

In our society the role of the father in childbirth is confused and ambiguous. In certain cultures he may have a well-defined and ritualized part to play, even in some tribes going through the pains of labor and delivery surrounded by sympathetic friends and relatives, while his wife has been sent outside the village to have the baby in isolation. In other cultures a man may be totally excluded from playing any part in the birth of his own child.

In Britain and the United States, with the advent of modern obstetrics, fathers were initially excluded from the hospital delivery room, on the grounds that they had no active medical part to play in life saving and were therefore an unhygienic, superfluous accessory who might get in the way of the specialist. As better social conditions have made childbirth safer and the death of the mother or baby has become less likely, the majority of births take place without mishap, thereby shifting the emphasis from mere physical survival to the emotional well-being of those concerned. Fathers are by no means always kept from the delivery room now.

It is easy to see how fathers may still feel excluded from the birth, even though actually present. Many prenatal clinics and programs have made an effort to involve the father actively, by teaching him how to help and support the mother during labor and delivery. The Charing Cross Hospital in London, for instance, a few years ago ran a program to teach husbands how to become more active participants in the labor. Of the first 730 husbands taking part, 61 percent were present throughout the whole of labor and 39 percent were present for part of it; 75 percent saw the baby being delivered and 99.6 percent said they were glad to be there; 92 percent thought their presence was beneficial. It is interesting to note that the social class of the men taking part in the study showed a strong bias toward the upper end.

Encouragement for fathers to be present during birth has only come in the last decade, and there are many places that still exclude them. Part of the reason has to do with the changing mechanics of technical obstetrics. In a recent study of induction, a random selection of one hundred mothers showed that fathers were present in only 18 percent of births, less than one in five. Closer analysis showed that more fathers were present in the noninduced control group than in the induced groups, and that the incidence of epidurals and forceps deliveries was also much higher in the induced groups. At the hospital where the study was done, it was the practice to move mothers from the normal delivery room to the operating theater if they needed forceps, and in general the fathers were excluded from the theater. So obstetrics, having reached the point of accepting the presence of fathers during delivery, altered its procedures and excluded them again.

In my study of the twelve deliveries, the father was present in six, and held the baby in three. The mothers spent about half as much time smiling at their husbands as they did at their newborn babies. From superficial observation of the videotapes, the husbands demonstrated great variation in the amount of direct support they showed their wives. But support can be given in many ways, and most of them are probably invisible to the camera. A study by W. J. Henneborn and R. Cogan showed that, when husbands attended special classes prior to birth and were present during delivery, this had a positive effect on their wives' reported feelings of pain, and decreased the use of medication.[6] It also markedly altered the couples' hindsight of the birth experience. In an unpublished study S. Tanzer compared deliveries where the husband was or was not present during the second stage of labor. Her findings show a striking effect of the husband's presence upon the wife's birth experience. In every case in which the women reported "raptures" and a "peak" of experience during birth, her husband had been with her in the delivery room.

There is an attempt today to break down the specific roles of men and women so that these roles can become interchangeable. Pregnancy, labor, and delivery will remain with the woman, should she want them, but it is not impossible to imagine that a man who is involved in helping his wife throughout pregnancy and labor, and who is present at delivery, shares in the moment, holds the child, and is immediately involved in the day-to-day routines of child care, will find it easier to continue this role later. A study from Sweden seems to support this idea.[7] Soon after their wives had delivered, a group of fathers went to the hospital twice to handle their babies and change their diapers. Follow-up at home showed that these fathers later spent more time with their infants than a control group of father who did not have this early experience.

There has been extensive research on the effects of childbirth on early mother-child relationships, but much remains to be learned about the early relationship of father and child, and also of father and mother.

TRANSCRIPT: MRS. B, AGED 27, FIRST BABY (A GIRL)

Father	Mother	Doctor
		Come on, junior. Only a lady could cause so much trouble. Come on, little one.
	(baby is delivered)	
	A girl.	Well, it's got the right plumbing.
	Oh I'm sorry, darling.	What are you sorry about?
	He wanted a boy.	Well, you'll have to try again next week, won't you!
(laughs)	*(laughs)*	She looks great. Want to see her? Bloody and messy, but that's not from her.
	Oh, she's gorgeous.	
	(mother kisses father)	
Looks like you.		Sorry, dear, I'm just going to need your cooperation for a moment. Will you move your

Father	Mother	Doctor
		bottom down the bed towards me—you've crept up the bed rather.
	Sorry. Do you want me to push?	
		Again please. No. A little more of your bottom down the bed.
	She's big, isn't she?	
		She's no Twiggy, this one.
	Seven pounds three you guessed.	
		Yes. I think I may have been a bit conservative.
	What do you think she is?	
		She's a bit more than that, I think.
Ooh!		
	Oh darling, how do you feel?	
		Relax your thighs, ma'am.
	(laughs)	
		Give me a cough.
	(coughs)	
	I'll stand on my head if you want me to now.	
		Not at all, dear.

(whispers to husband)

We've had to make a little cut, as we often do, but I don't think you'll feel it, and I'll just stitch that up right away. Do you feel it?

Yes.

It's just the afterbirth now.

Is she all right?

Why don't you ask her? She's quite capable of letting you know how she feels about the situation.

She's noisy, isn't she?

Yes, just like the modern generation.

Well, Dr. Murphy, I was right. I had a sneaky feeling it was a girl, just because I wanted a boy.

(laughs)

Well, it will suit your mum, won't it?

Yes.

Often tactically best to have a girl first—she can help with the washing up.

Father	Mother	Doctor
	(baby given to mother)	
	Hello darling. Meet your dad. You're just like your dad *(baby yells)*.	
I'm going home!		
	Oh you've gone quiet *(laughs)*. Oh darling, she's just like you—she's got your little tiny nose.	
It'll grow like yours.		
	She's big, isn't she? What do you reckon?	
		She's quite good-looking, despite forceps marks on her head— but don't worry about that. She'll have little bruises around her ears—well, they usually have. I don't know if she does.
	There's one—there . . . Oh look, she's got hair. It's a girl—you're supposed to be all little.	
		What do you think she weighs, Richard? I think about seven and a half.

Gosh. Oh, she's lovely. Oh, she's opened her eyes (*laughs*). Oh lovely (*kisses baby*).

She's a little bit bloody and messy, but that's from where I made the cut to help her out, and none of it's from her, so no need for concern.

Oh, she's gorgeous, she's lovely. She's got blue eyes. You hold her. Come on.

No.

Why not? (*laughs*) You're all of a tremble, aren't you?

I dropped the first one I held.

Charming!

Oh look, oh mine. Hello darling. Good lungs, hasn't she? She's got a dimple—where'd she get that from?

That's probably from the forceps. Actually, have you got dimples?

Father	Mother	Doctor
		Oh, she's in great nick.
	Oh no, neither of us have. Oh, you're lovely. Look . . . She's lovely. I thought she'd be all mauve and crinkly.	
	Yes. I was expecting her to be all mauve and shrivelled, but she's not, is she?	Not at all. In front of the cameras she's a real lady.
	Oh dear. Having your photo taken, darling? Oh.	Ma'am, can I ask you to drop your ankles apart?
	She doesn't go much on this (*nurse attaching name-tag to baby*).	
Like British Rail, labelling her like a parcel.	Oh look, darling, look at the size of her feet. She's got no toenails.	What do you mean, she hasn't got any toenails?

She hasn't got any toenails.
They're soft.

I don't think you'd like it
if she was scratching around
inside you.

Look—fabulous. Aren't you
pleased with her?

Yes, of course.

You said that if it was a
girl it could go back.

I'm not putting her back.

Well, it came from him in
the first place.

Back to the manufacturers, yes.

Quite. (*kisses the baby
and laughs*)

It's his spermatozoa that
decides the sex.

You'll imagine her going out
with all sorts of blokes
like you were. (*laughs*)
In a sort of odd way I was
after his money really.

I shall be worried to
death when she's
eighteen.

All two quid. Go, go to dad.

Yes?

Father	Mother	Doctor
No, she doesn't want to.		Come on, the generation gap can't be showing so soon.
	Yes she does.	
No she doesn't.		
	Go on, cuddle her, she won't bite you. Don't be silly, of course she won't.	
Are you sure?		
	Yes, go on—she won't hurt.	
I don't know how it's done.		
	(baby given to father)	
	It doesn't really matter. They're built like rubber anyway at that stage.	
Well, she's not cleaned yet.		
	She's a bit yukky and revolting, but she's rather sweet. It's a jolly good job they do. I suppose you've decided that's what you always wanted to do in the first place. Why?	
	(baby given back to mother)	

Oh, you're lovely. Well, what do you think, love? Can you see her? Oh, she has got a long neck. You look as though you feel exhausted.

(father jokingly handed gas by doctor)

(laughs) It's not gas I want, It's a triple brandy.

Quick whiff. I know what you want and that is a fag.

Haven't you been able to have one?

Oh dear, fancy wanting a nice fag.

Yes. Yes. Well, painful, but I don't particularly care at this stage. She's opened her eyes. They're not—they're dark blue. Don't say they're brown— we haven't got brown eyes in either family.

Sorry, ma'am, I'm putting needles in a part where you're not numb. Am I hurting you?

Father	Mother	Doctor
		They're always blue in the beginning and find their own colour later.
	God, it doesn't . . . Doing a lovely piece of darning down there?	
		Plastic surgery of the first order.
	How splendid. Well, if you look in the book case at home, in the right hand book case, hidden behind the bible is a bottle of Tia Maria.	
	It's the place he wouldn't look. Oh dear.	Behind the bible!
		I'm sorry.

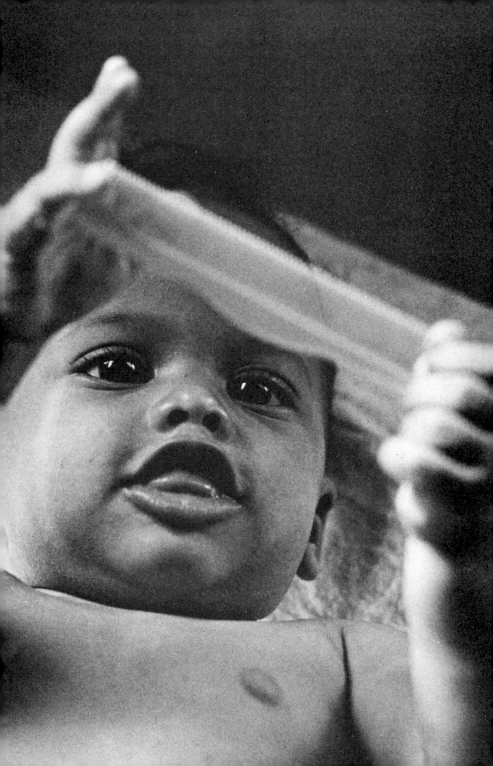

6 / What the Baby Knows

It has come as more of a surprise to psychologists than to mothers (though the two of course are not mutually exclusive) that babies, after nine months of development in the uterus, are born so highly organized. They are born with a great number of automatic reflexes, performed in response to appropriate stimulation: they grasp objects put in the palm of their hands; they attempt to crawl if put face downward on a firm surface; they extend and flex their arms rapidly if their heads are let drop a short distance; they purse their lips if the base of the thumb is lighly stroked; they curve their backs when scratched down one side of the spine; they make stepping movements with the foot if the back of the foot is firmly stroked with the leg is extended; they turn their heads when the side of the mouth is touched. They are also able to select and use a great deal of information from their surroundings, and they show a wide range of behavior to demonstrate their needs in both subtle and forceful ways.

At one time it was thought that a newborn baby received all sensations from the environment, with no selectivity or discrimination. But this is not so, not by far. Although we are still discovering just how competent the newborn baby is, it is obvious that, just by being born human, the infant fresh out from his mother's womb already has the ability to be attracted to the features of another human being. This is remarkable because he has had no previous experience of the sight or sound of human beings from the outside.

How do we know what babies can see, hear, or feel? How can we tell that they are more attracted to one thing than to another, when they are so tiny? There are many ways of finding out, some more complicated than others. We might simply watch the baby and carefully note all the things he does in a fifteen-second period in every minute for an hour, or we might record the baby's heartbeat and breathing rhythm to see if they change when something happens to the baby. We might also build a highly complicated piece of machinery which, say, shines a light into the baby's eyes so that it reflects from the backs of the eyes into a television camera; this produces a picture on a screen which can be automatically analyzed by computer to show what exactly the baby is looking at. These are just a few examples of how observations are made, but undoubtedly the most pleasant is that used by mothers when trying to find out what their babies are thinking—watching them very carefully. One of the masters at baby watching is Peter Wolff. He studied a group of ten babies in their own homes, each for thirty hours per week.[1] He was particularly interested in the amount of time the babies spent in an attentive state, when they have "a general disposition to respond adaptively to selected elements in a constantly changing environment." In this state the baby is fully awake, breathing evenly, with eyes wide open, and quiet. The time he spends like this increases over the weeks, from 11 percent in the first week to 21 percent by the fourth. The rest of the time he is either drowsy, asleep, or crying. Wolff also observed that with this group of infants, during the first six hours immediately after birth the amount of alert inactivity varied greatly from infant to infant: some stayed awake for an hour and a half before the first sleep and did not have another alert period of equal length until the end of the first month; others fell asleep within fifteen minutes of delivery and would only wake up fully on the second or third day.

The reason I mention this here is that a baby's reactions to the changing environment greatly depend on the state he is in. It is common now, when making observations, to divide the baby's degree of "awakeness" into six possible categories: (1) deep sleep, with regular breathing, (2) light sleep, with irregular breathing and occasional restlessness, (3) drowsy, (4) awake, eyes open, but quiet rather than excited, (5) awake, eyes open, but moving actively, and (6) crying. (Some researchers use only five categories, dividing [3] between [2] and [4].[2])

The best time to observe the baby's reactions to different

sights, sounds, and smells is when he is alert, in state 4. Unfortunately, as Wolff's study suggests, the time the baby spends like this in the first few days is very short. There are ways to improve our chances for good observation, however. First we can observe the babies at certain times of day, since there is evidence that babies spend more time alert just before or after feeds. This is not always true, though; just before a feeding the baby may be too hungry and start crying if not fed immediately. After a feeding he may drop off to sleep. The extent of this period of alertness seems to depend as well on whether the babies are being demand-fed or schedule-fed. If we choose to observe a baby just before he is fed, we can stop him from crying and keep him in an apparently alert state by getting him to suck on a blind teat. But the very act of sucking in itself alters the way in which he reacts to the environment, since babies have difficulty in dividing their attention between two things—for instance, between sucking and looking. Paul Harris and I did a study to see how far sideways a baby would look if we presented him with a flashing light nine inches away and starting in the periphery of his vision. The degree to which babies responded was much greater if they were not sucking.[3]

For many tests the best time is between meals, when babies are not yet hungry for their next meal. At this time a baby is usually sleeping, and he has to be waked up with great gentleness and care, by talking to him, very slowly turning him over, hesitantly removing his clothing, and so on; as much or even more care is needed to keep him in an alert state once he is awake. All those who try and observe the baby's reactions to different specific things know the patience needed and the frustrations involved.

Many other factors affect a baby's state of alertness. Heinz Prechtl gathered evidence from the brain-wave patterns of very small babies that they were never fully awake under two weeks of age if they were lying flat on their backs, but were much more alert if they were lying at an angle, with their heads higher than their feet, or were fully upright.[4] We probably all have noticed how alert babies seem when they are held up against the shoulder, and during breastfeeding the head is held higher than the legs. Originally, many psychologists did test babies when they were flat on their backs, and got negative results. But in some cases, when they repeated the tests with the babies sitting up, the babies responded, and today we frequently use small supportive chairs, inclined at an angle, for babies to sit in. Other factors affecting response include the temperature of the surroundings: too hot and the baby goes off to sleep, too cold and he starts crying. Touch also matters: if the baby is tightly swaddled, he tends to go to sleep, but he may become distressed if totally naked. Light is an influence: too much and he shuts his eyes with a grimace, too dim and he may go to sleep again.

If the baby is to respond to certain things in the outside world he needs to encounter certain features or stimuli that attract his attention, and he has to link them up to his previous experiences. If the stimulus is too intense, too bright, too noisy, or has too many novel features, then he may defend himself—show withdrawal behavior such as turning away or crying. If the intensity of the stimulus is too low or too familiar, then he may ignore it. These changes of behavior seem to be accompanied by changes in heartrate. If the baby is interested and attentive to an event, then his heartbeat tends to slow down. If the stimulus is too intense or frightening, then his heart speeds up, perhaps in preparation for defense of some sort.

SEEING

It is quite easy to observe that the newborn baby can appreciate brightness and that he does not like very bright lights. Even with the eyes closed and when he is asleep, he will screw up his eyes, frown, and tense his muscles if a bright light is suddenly shone directly into his face. If, however, he is awake and is brought near a window, provided he is not directly in sunlight he will often turn toward the light, indicating that he knows where it is and is attracted by it. It would seem possible that if one shone a bright light on the pregnant mother's tummy sometime before delivery, the baby might turn toward it, and perhaps some of the baby's movements before birth stem from this.

But after he is born, a baby is very much more discriminating. If you move your head slowly backward and forward nine inches away from his face, he may follow it for short distances, with jerky eye movements. To discover which features of the human face a baby preferred to look at, Robert Fantz showed a series of babies three flat objects, all in the size and shape of a head.[5] On the first was painted a regular stylized face in black on a pink background. The second had the same features as the first, but scrambled, and on the third was painted a solid black patch at one end, equal in area to the features of the first two. The babies he tested were aged from four days old to six months, but the results showed that, at all ages, they looked most at the real face, somewhat less at the scrambled face, and least at the third object with the black patch.

Most of the studies on what babies prefer to look at have involved presenting them with two things at the same time and observing their eye movements to see which one they look at more. This method has shown that babies are attracted by contrast. They like complex patterns in which there is a great deal of sharp demarcation. It is therefore not surprising that they are found to watch particularly the eyes of the human face, for with their whites, darker irises, and black pupils, the eyes present definite contrasts. It is obviously interesting and significant that infants should be attracted to eyes and faces as they are.

Preference studies of this sort have also been used to judge how good a baby's eyesight is.[6] Since a baby prefers looking at contours or contrast rather than at, say, a gray field, one can present him with pairs of cards, each showing black and white lines of equal width. On successive different cards for comparison, the black and white lines grow narrower and narrower. At a certain point one card will appear to the baby as an all-gray blur, when the lines are so narrow that they cannot be seen individually. When this happens the baby will show a preference for the other, whose slightly wider lines he can see clearly. This point seems to be reached at cards with lines one eighth of an inch wide.

It was not realized until recently that very small babies could see at all, because it had not been discovered that they have a fairly rigid distance of focus, at somewhere around nine inches. If you want a baby to look at something, it is best to show it to him at this distance—which is incidentally just about the same distance the mother's face is from her baby's when she is breast-feeding. Recent work shows that this distance may not be completely fixed, for by examining the movements of each eye individually, and the distance between the center of the pupils, we can observe that the eyes converge and diverge when babies

look at objects ten to twenty inches away, but that they don't
when the objects are nearer or farther off.[7] This strongly suggests that babies do see objects within this range, but not outside
it. (This effect of convergence is exactly what happens if you
watch a finger moving toward or away from your nose.) In the
study mentioned, the eye movements were analyzed from film.
If, however, we observe the baby's eyes directly, with no special
technique, convergence can't be detected before the child is
twenty weeks old.

Tom Bower wanted to measure the newborn baby's expectation that an object would be solid.[8] He filmed the reactions of a
series of babies, aged less than two weeks, while a large object
was moved at different speeds toward them. Examining the films
he found that, as the object approached, the babies pulled their
heads back and put their hands between them and the object.
This shows that they already have a reaction that would defend
them against getting hit by the object, and implies that they expect it to be solid. The reaction was specific for objects ap-
proaching at a certain speed and on a "hit path," for if the object
moved away from or to one side of the baby, or if the speed of
approach changed, then he did not react. Another experiment
that Bower did was to create the optical illusion of an object by
using polaroid light. If the baby was sitting up in a special supportive chair so that his arms and hands were free to move, he
appeared to try and grasp an object if it was presented as within
reach. If it was an illusory object and he tried to grasp it only to
find that it wasn't there, he was greatly disturbed. This, then,
seems to indicate that at least one aspect of the coordination
between eye and hand is present at birth. The baby expects to
feel what he can see.

The most common of the more complicated sights a baby sees
after birth is his mother's face, not as a still object in one plane,
like a photograph, but as a dynamic and continually moving
object with varied expressions and different associated contexts,
such as food and warmth. How soon does the baby come to distinguish his mother's face from others? Genevieve Carpenter sat
two-week-old babies in supportive chairs and, when they were
alert, presented them with either their mother's face or a strange
mother's face in an opening in a frame in front of them.[9] She
observed the babies' general behavior, where they looked and

for how long. At two weeks the babies spent a longer time looking at their own mother's face than they did at the stranger's face. In fact, when they were presented with the strange mother's face, they frequently showed strong gaze aversion, looking right away almost over their shoulders. This kind of withdrawal suggests that the babies found the stimulus too intense or too novel.

HEARING

It is obvious to most mothers that their babies can hear. If the baby is alert, then a loud noise, such as a door slamming, will usually make him tense up or startle. However, we should remember that during the first few days after birth the middle part of the ear behind the eardrum is still full of amniotic fluid, and that this only gradually gets absorbed or evaporates. Until it is, sounds reaching the baby's ear are dampened.

I have already mentioned a study by Michael Wertheimer, who sounded clicks at one or other of a newborn's ears and noted that he turned his eyes toward the clicks.[10] At four days of age or even younger, a baby can be taught to turn his head one way for a bell and the other way for a buzzer, by rewarding him when he is right. But there is a great deal more that we know about the baby's hearing. Recently there has been considerable work done on the response to sound inside the uterus very early in labor. This has been made possible by putting a very small microphone on the end of a catheter and inserting it into the uterus after the membranes have broken; it is placed close to the baby's ear and can record the noise actually reaching him. Since it is possible as well to record his heartrate at this stage, we can produce a loud noise at the mother's tummy wall, and both record it from inside the uterus and see what effects it has on the heartrate. It seems from this, and from work done with babies right after birth, that "patterned" sounds produce more response than pure tones, and that the most effective sound of all is one that includes the fundamental frequencies found in the human voice. There is also evidence from research done by John Hutt that babies respond better to the higher frequencies.[11] In the light of this, it is interesting that both mothers and fathers often talk to their babies in high-pitched voices but return to normal as soon as they talk to another adult again. It is also true that if one holds a baby up and has a man talk to it normally from one side and a woman from the other, the baby seems to turn more frequently to the woman. If the woman is the mother, it seems as if the baby is actually recognizing her. And this may in fact be so, for another study shows that if a mother consistently calls her baby by name every time she picks him up, or feeds him or is near him, then by the third day, if she stands out of the baby's line of sight and calls his name, he will frequently turn toward her. If a strange mother does the same thing, the baby is much less likely to respond.

A more controlled study of this kind was done by Margaret Mills.[12] She tested babies who were between twenty and thirty days of age, and arranged things so that when they sucked on a teat, they heard a recording of either their own mother's or a strange mother's voice, both matched for loudness. She found that the babies would suck significantly more to conjure up the sound of their own mother. So this is another subtle difference in babies' behavior toward mothers and strangers.

I have already talked about the baby's ability to tell whether a sound comes from the right or the left, as indicated by eye movements. It is suggested that one way that he can tell which side a sound is coming from is because the sound waves reach one ear before the other, and because different parts of the waves reach the two ears. In order to locate a sound, a baby might turn his head so that the sound reaching the two ears is equal. This is all somewhat confused by some studies which suggest that the two ears do not appreciate sound equally: quiet sounds played at the left ear do not affect the direction of the eye movements as much as they do if played at the right ear, and it is therefore possible that the two ears may have different thresholds of sensitivity.[13]

Turning the eyes toward a sound is certainly quite sophisticated, but five-day-old babies seem to be able to do even better than this. If instead of eye-turning we look at the baby's patterns of head-turning, we find that to a certain extent he seems to be able to tell from what angle a sound is coming. For instance, babies will turn their heads more toward a sound coming from an angle of 80 degrees from the midline than toward a sound coming from 15 degrees from the midline on the same side.

It also seems that if you turn your face backward and forward in front of the baby's face without talking, he tends to follow you with jerky eye movements, and only starts making head movements when his eyes can no longer continue the tracking by themselves. If, however, you talk to him at the same time, head movements seem to begin almost simultaneously with the eye movements—as if he were trying to keep the sound coming from a position between his two ears. Occasionally I have observed babies who under these conditions make no eye movements at all, but simply track the face by holding the eyes straight ahead and moving the head only.

Finally there are the intriguing findings of William Condon, who for many years analyzed films of adults talking to one another. He found that people talking seemed to move in synchrony with speech. This "dance" can only be detected by careful film analysis, when even the very smallest movements can be examined. Condon and Louis Sander later joined in a project of videotaping a series of infants aged between twelve hours and two days old, and they showed that even at this incredibly early age the babies seem to move in precise time to human speech. They did so whether the speech they heard was in English or Chinese.[14]

SMELL

Smell is another of the senses by which we gather information about other people and the world around. Our sense of smell is not particularly good when compared with many animals, but we are nevertheless capable of considerable discrimination between smells, and many of us find smells very evocative. It seems that smell is a fairly old sense in terms of our evolutionary development and is associated with parts of the brain which are themselves phylogenetically ancient.

We all have body smells (a fact some of us consider unfortunate) which are as unique to us as our fingerprints. Related people have related smells. Bloodhounds know this, for a hound after sniffing a man is more likely to follow the track of that man's brother than of some stranger. It is also possible that we emit subtle smells that influence the behavior of others, without any of us knowing it. For instance, the fact that women living in the same institution after a while come to menstruate at the same time may be due to the influence of smells, and the smell of a

woman during ovulation may have strange effects on the con-
centration of men around here. It is also significant that we tend
to use smells more during close body contact, as when making
love, and this may well be true during the course of early
mother-baby contact.

That very small babies can smell has been shown by Engen,
Lipsitt, and Kay, who observed the activity, heartrate, and
breathing patterns of twenty babies aged two days.[15] Each baby
was presented with two smells chosen from anise oil, asafetida,
acetic acid, or phenyl alcohol. When a smell was initially presented to the baby, he changed his activity, heartrate, and
breathing patterns. If the smell continued, the baby gradually
learned to take no notice of it (habituation), but as soon as the
smell was changed to a new one, then up went the activity and
heartrate and breathing patterns changed again—the infant
recognized the smell as being different from the one he had
become used to.

Recently I have done several studies with small babies to test
just how sensitive their sense of smell is.[16] I had noticed that
sometimes when a baby is put to his mother's breast, he turns his
face to the breast even before he has looked at it or before his
face has been touched by the nipple. This might have been due
to his sensing the heat of the breast, and indeed infra-red photo-
graphs show that the two breasts and the lips of a lactating
woman are her warmest areas of skin. It might also be that the
baby learns very rapidly that when one side of his body is held
against his mother he has to turn his head to that side to get fed.
However, the baby might also be smelling the breast, for each
time the baby is fed he will have his nose in close contact with the
breast, so that the food and the smell may become closely associated.

What I did initially was to take a breast pad (a piece of gauze
measuring four inches square) which had been inside the mother's bra between feeds, and put it at one side of the baby's head,
touching his cheek. At the same time, I put a clean breast pad on
the other side against the cheek and for one minute filmed all the
movements of the baby's head; at the end of the minute I reversed the pads for another minute. Several previous studies had
shown that babies tend spontaneously to turn their heads more
to the right than the left, perhaps because mothers tend to put

their babies more often on their own left. Analysis of the films showed that at five days of age the babies were spending more time with their heads turned toward their mother's pad than to the clean pad. To get more subtle results I repeated the test but used another mother's breast pad instead of a clean one. At two days of age the babies spent an equal amount of time with both pads; but at six days the babies were generally spending more time turned to their own mother's pad than to the strange mother's pad. At ten days of age this effect was even more striking. All the babies were being breast-fed and were tested when they were most hungry, that is, just before a feeding. This still left open the question of whether it was the breast milk itself, the mother's smell, or a combination of the two that attracted the baby. So I did one further experiment, which revealed that babies do not turn toward breast milk on its own—perhaps the smell of the milk is not strong enough. Here again we witness the ability of the baby to distinguish his own mother from strange mothers at only six days of age. But frequently, when I told mothers I was doing a study to see if their babies could smell them, they rushed off, saying they must put on some deodorant. It was all I could do to dissuade them.

Perhaps smell also has an effect on the mother's behavior. In a pilot study we got a series of mothers to sniff their babies. We blindfolded the mothers and got them to wear earphones so they could neither see nor hear their babies. If they were given a choice of two babies to smell, a significant number managed to identify their own, though I suspect they may have been using other clues. Other observations related to smell are that babies who have been breast-fed and then changed to a bottle change their smell; this is probably due to an alteration in the smell of their excreta—the breast-fed baby's excreta are rather sweet-smelling, whereas the bottle-fed's are more like an adult's. It also seems that mothers become well adapted to the smell of their own baby's excreta but get nauseated at other babies'.

TASTE AND THE BREAST-BOTTLE ARGUMENT

Taste on its own is a relatively simple sense in human beings, and the finer discriminations that we think we can make by taste we actually make by smell.

There are two observations that indicate that the baby inside the uterus is able to taste. In the first chapter I described how the baby surrounded by fluid swallows it continually and then pees it out again, and there is evidence that the baby may actually control the amount of fluid around him. In certain pregnancies too much fluid sometimes accumulates too fast, and forty years ago a doctor developed a novel way of treating this. He injected saccharine into the amniotic fluid in order to sweeten it, and he found that he could thereby reduce the amount of fluid, possibly by having encouraged the baby to swallow more. More recently another doctor found that injecting a substance opaque to X-rays into the amniotic fluid caused a decrease in swallowing; this was clear from the X-ray pictures of the substance being swallowed by the child. The opaque substance he had injected was known to have an extremely unpleasant taste. All this suggests that a fetus can taste.

Louis Lipsitt and his colleagues have been looking at the effect of altering the sweetness of a feed on the baby's sucking patterns and on his heartrate.[17] Taking babies two to three days old, they arranged a system by which, each time the baby sucked, he got a minute fixed amount of fluid. This fluid contained varying amounts of sugar. They found that the more sugar there was in the solution, the slower the baby sucked and the more the heartrate increased. This is in some ways not what one would expect: certainly I would have thought that if the baby tasted a sweet substance he would have sucked faster to try and get more. In this case, however, where the baby was getting only a very small and fixed amount with each suck, he sucked more slowly; this should mean that less effort was used and the heart should have slowed down, but it did not—which is all very paradoxical. One explanation that Lipsitt put forward is that the sucking rate is slowed to make it easier for the baby to savor the sweeter fluid, and that perhaps the excitement of tasting a different and more concentrated fluid increases the heartrate. It is probable, though, that it is all more complicated than this.

Fascinating too are the results of work done by David Salisbury.[18] He was looking at the effects of different feeds on babies' swallowing, sucking, and breathing patterns. Previous work had shown that water, cow's milk, and glucose, when introduced into the back of a calf's throat, interrupted its breathing, while a salt-water solution did not; this suggested that a calf has specialized taste receptors to prevent it from breathing when swallowing. Salisbury looked at the effects of feeding different solutions to human babies, and he found that, when given salt water, they suppressed breathing very poorly. When he fed them sterile water, however, none inhaled it—which suggests that a baby may also have these specialized taste receptors. Using a specially designed bottle, Salisbury also examined the breathing, sucking, and swallowing patterns of the infants when fed artificial milk or breast milk. Again the patterns were different for the two types.

It is known that the composition of breast milk alters as to the time of day and as to how far through a feeding the baby is. At the beginning breast milk is rather diluted; it becomes more concentrated toward the end. So the baby gets his fluids at the beginning and his food at the end. Shifting from one breast to another has been likened to having a drink in the middle of a meal.

The issue of breast- versus bottle-feeding, like those of induction and home delivery, has been highly contentious, because it highlights the economic, cultural, social, psychological, and physiological influences at work on human behavior. On the simplest level, human breast milk is produced by humans for humans and has developed over the course of human existence; it contains certain substances, and not others, for purposes we are only just becoming aware of. Most mothers can breastfeed given the right chance, and a small number cannot.

Breastfeeding is associated with a lower incidence of intestinal infection in the baby, a lower incidence of milk allergies, better protection against certain diseases, owing to the transfer of antibodies from the mother through her milk, and better protection against malnutrition or overfeeding, which can occur with artificial feeds. There is also evidence that the incidence of crib death is lower among breast-fed babies. As suggested by Salisbury's study, the incidence of inhalation of feeds into the lungs should be negligible on breast milk but might occur with artificial feeds if they contained certain concentrations of salt.

Psychological reasons for breastfeeding include the satisfaction that the mother might get from feeling that she is continuing to support and nourish the child from her own body. Her baby will be held so that his face is nine inches away from hers, and as a result of his inclined position he will probably be fairly alert. The baby is also more likely to be held right up against the mother's body during the feeding.

Factors affecting the success or failure of breastfeeding have been suggested by Martin Richards and Judy Bernal.[19] They found that breast-fed babies seemed to cry more than those fed by bottle. The mothers in their study had been advised by medical personnel to feed their babies every four hours, although it is thought that the amount of protein in breast milk may only be enough to keep a baby from hunger for three hours. In response to their babies' cries, one group of mothers tended to give up, believing they could not produce enough milk. A second group continued to breastfeed, but fed more often. Interestingly, the first group of mothers tended to come from a lower social class than the second group, and the investigators suggested that the mothers who gave up were more responsive to the specific instruction they had received from the doctor, midwife, or nurse; the others had chosen to ignore this advice in the light of their own experience that feeding the baby more often stopped him from getting hungry.

The cultural and economic aspects of breastfeeding are now receiving publicity. In many Third World countries, where until recently breastfeeding was the norm, bottle feeding is becoming more common, apparently in response to Western cultural influences. This has been accompanied by an increase in the incidence of infection, overfeeding, and illness from incorrectly prepared milk. There is also a widespread suspicion that manufacturers' advertising and promotion of artificial feeding have in some cases been motivated more by the idea of profit than by the actual benefits they might bring to mothers and babies. Other special, cultural, and economic factors—such as a woman's need to go back to work after giving birth—obviously have an influence as well.

FEELING PAIN

We still accept the idea that newborn babies do not feel as much pain as they do later, as demonstrated by the continuing practice in the United States of circumcising newborn babies without anesthetics. If it were necessary to remove an equivalent area of highly sensitive skin from some other part of the body, say the little finger, I think most people would be horrified if it were done without an anesthetic; and yet few demand this for circumcision.

Little systematic research has been done on the baby's perceptions of pain, which is all to the good since no one wants to hurt babies deliberately simply to find out how they react. It does not take psychological research to indicate that babies do feel pain. Direct observation of any baby who has to have a blood test shows us that. Blood samples are commonly obtained by pricking the baby's heel with a small stylette and collecting the drops in a container. The normal reaction of a baby to this procedure is immediately to try and withdraw his foot and to wail with anguish. He may also tense all his muscles and turn a bright red. If we were recording his heartbeat and breathing patterns, we would find that these change rapidly as well. But the reaction varies greatly from baby to baby, depending both on his individual temperament and on his state of alertness at the time. And the reactions of the baby to pain can be modified—for instance, the heartrate increases after circumcision can be reduced by having the baby suck at the same time.

It has been observed that a newborn baby's sleep patterns are disturbed after a heel prick, and this also proves to be so after circumcision. In one study the disturbance followed very soon after circumcision; in a second study there was a prolonged period of wakefulness and fussing, which was then followed by an increase in quiet sleep states. Circumcision has also been put forward as the cause of some of the sex differences that have been noted in studies of newborn babies. Most of these studies have been done in the United States on a population where the majority of males are circumcised at birth. It may be that some differences between male and female babies are due to this procedure rather than to any innate differences.[20]

Babies who have to go into special-care units after birth because they are very small or sick undergo a large number of unpleasant procedures: repeated blood tests, intravenous drips, tubes down their throats to help them breathe. These are obviously unavoidable, but they may affect the way the baby behaves for a time afterward.

TOUCH AND TEMPERATURE

The baby at birth has a large number of reflex responses to being touched at different spots. Most of these are already present when he is in the uterus, and some will disappear soon after birth. The rooting reflex, for instance, occurs when the baby's cheek is touched to one side of the mouth: he turns his head toward the touch. If the baby's palm is touched, he will close his fingers as if to grip. If the back of his foot is touched firmly, he may bend his leg at the knee and hip and then straighten it out again, the so-called placing reflex. If the baby is stroked firmly down the back just to one side of the spine, he will curve his back in to the side being stroked—this has been called the salamander reflex because of its similarity to the back movements of a salamander when it is walking. We do not yet have explanations for many of these touch reflexes. The rooting reflex obviously serves to bring a nipple touching the cheek in direct contact with the mouth so that it can be sucked on—but why the salamander reflex?

Another observation that shows the baby's responsiveness to touch can be made when he is lying in a crib and crying but not hungry. It is often enough simply to place a hand firmly on his chest or tummy to get him to stop. Other more controlled studies were done of babies' behavior when being undressed, as well as the effects of blowing air at them. Girls, for some reason, react much more strongly than boys.

Temperature control in babies is very delicate, and they tend to lose heat rapidly. They do have special reserves of fat under the skin around the shoulders, which can be used to help make extra heat and maintain a steady temperature. Simple observation makes it clear that temperature affects a baby's behavior: warm babies who are not hungry tend to go off to sleep while cold ones cry.

RHYTHMS

I have already mentioned the quieting effect on a baby of playing a recording of a heart beating at about 60-80 beats a minute. A light flashing at the same rhythm will have a similar effect. Another kind of rhythmical stimulation has been studied by Anthony Ambrose and Louis Lipsitt.[21] They designed a special crib that could be rocked automatically at varying speeds, and they found, not surprisingly, that the optimal speed was 60 rocks a minute. By studying the various lengths and direction of rock, they showed that the most effective was an up-and-down movement of about three inches which began and ended gradually with a fast phase in the middle, like a pendulum in a vertical plane.

Ambrose and Lipsett also found that babies have another kind of rhythmicity. If they gave a baby ten-second periods of rocks at 60 per minute, followed by periods of 20 seconds with no rocking, then each time the rocking began the baby's heartrate and breathing patterns changed. If the periods of rocking were stopped, each time a period of rocking *should* have begun, the baby's heartrate and breathing still showed changes, as if in anticipation. This continued for several minutes after the periods of rocking had stopped.

These studies reveal two new kinds of appreciation of rhythms. One comes from stimulation of that part of the ear called the vestibular mechanism, which is responsible for balance and by which we can tell which way up we are in space. The other is that of periodicity, whereby a baby is able to anticipate a future rhythmic experience from a past one.

IMITATION

If there is one ability that more than any other demonstrates the sophistication of newborn babies, it is that of imitation. In a series of beautifully controlled studies, Andrew Meltzov, working in both England and the United States, has demonstrated that children of two weeks can stick their tongues out or clench and unclench their hands when they watch someone else do these things. This can only be detected by very close analysis of videotape and film and is not immediately obvious to the eye.

The baby in this sort of imitation has to watch another person sticking out a tongue; he then has to realize that his own tongue is equivalent to the other person's, in spite of the fact that he has never seen his own tongue. Without being able to see what he is doing himself, he must match his movements to the ones he does see. These studies are very recent and are likely to have considerable impact on theories of social development in children.

TRANSCRIPT: MRS. C, AGED 25, FIRST BABY (A BOY)

Father	Mother	Midwife
		Look—more, more, more.
	I can't see.	
	(baby is delivered)	
	Oh, ah, ah, ah. Ahahah.	
		Oh my goodness me.
	Oh. Oh, it's a boy. Ah. Ah. Oh dear. Oh, oh. Oh, no. *(during this period, the baby is lying between mother's legs— mother appears ecstatic)*	
	(father kisses and hugs wife)	
	Ah. He . . . he . . . *(laughs)*. Oh.	
		He's gorgeous.
	Oh, no wonder he was kicking like mad.	
Yes.		
		I think that's calling him 'him'.
	Oh, it's a beautiful boy. Oh poppet.	
(laughs)		

(laughs)

Oh.

We've been waiting such
a long time.

Oh (laughs) look at him.

Come on, love, sit up for a
second. You can have him
in a mo. Super girl.

Look at his size—smashing,
isn't he.

Smashing when they come out,
isn't it? Amazing when they
come out, isn't it?

(baby given to mother)

Oh, oh. Oh. Oh look at his
little mouth.

(laughs)

Oh. Oh.

It's lovely. Look at his little
face. His little nails.
Oh. His little squashed-up
nose like your nose (to father).
He has red hair.

(laughs and nods agreement)

He hasn't got red hair.

Father	Mother	Midwife
	It's as red as red.	We were wrong you know, weren't we?
(laughs)	Oh. Oh, oh, oh. Look . . .	
Little baby got big feet— he has got big feet, hasn't he?		
	Oh, ah.	She sounds as if she has run a four-minute mile.
	Oh, his cheeks are coming rosy, love.	
		Just give me another push. Bend that leg up and see if you can push the placenta out. Push. Push down against my hand. Push. Come on, push again. OK—rest for a second.
	Look at his little head. Look at his little mouth.	
(laughs) Look at his hand. I bet it's as tiring for him as it is for you.	He's gone to sleep. I wonder whether he was sucking his	

Amazing sight.

thumb inside. He knows his
face, look (*baby touching his
face with a hand*). Oh get off
(*baby appears to swipe away
father's touching fingers*).

                         He can't be ten pounds.

You said eight pounds.
I said nine pounds.

Ah, I can't believe it.

It's red, isn't it. It's
fair round the side too.

Look at his hair. Oh look,
it's all fair there.

                         It's very difficult to tell.
                         It's red round the top there.

He is going a nice colour
now, aren't you (*to baby*)?
He's sucking his thumb.
How any man can feel sick
at it, I don't know (*referring
to men feeling sick when
present at birth*).

I think the thought is, yes.

Oh you poppet. It wasn't bad.

                         Isn't it ghastly?

                         You were terrific, especially when
                         we had some delays. You did

Father	Mother	Midwife
		awfully well. (*to baby*) Stupid child, I don't know what you were getting up to inside— having a whale of a time.
	He was, wasn't he?	He came out the right way round. He had turned right round the proper way.
	Oh dear, what did you do that for (*to indistinguishable action by baby*)? He's blowing bubbles. His little hands are all wrinkled—looks like he's done the washing up, doesn't he?	
Yes (*laughs*). Oh dear!		So doesn't he look nice?
Oh dear!	He looks . . .	
		It was a girl you were so sure about?
Yes. Every day we had a different idea. That was the trouble.	No. *We* knew it was going to be a boy, didn't we (*to husband*)?	

That's why it's a boy. Open your eyes then (to the baby). Ahh (laughs). Can you open your eyes then? He's scratched himself by the look of it, on his face.

No, that's just blood that he brought with him. Give a little push down, love. Give a good push right down into my hand.

Oh (pain with contraction of third stage of labour).

You're not squeezing him too hard, are you?

No, he's resting on me.

Can you do one more? Come on— here it comes.

Hello (as baby opens his eyes for the first time)!

Oh, he's going (imitates baby blinking). Hello (laughs).

Don't distract her. She's meant to be pushing.

Baby is straining away too.

Oh, he's opened his eyes. there—look, look.

Sorry.

Father	Mother	Midwife
	Oh, his eyes are all stuck. Hello.	
(*laughs*) What colour are they?		
Oh yeah!	Dark blue.	
		Come on, here it comes (*hoping for delivery of placenta*).
	Hello, look. He's got your eyes (*to husband*). Look, you've got beautiful blue eyes (*to baby*). What are you looking at me like that for (*to baby*)?	
(*laughs*) Yes, but they're blind, you know.		
	Hello. Oh, he's got a beautiful face. Yah (*delivery of placenta*). How long do they usually take to open their eyes?	
		Oh, it varies. Has he opened them now?
	He's got one open now.	
		Another injection coming now. It's a stingy one.
	We will have to give you a	

(laughs) Well I'm blowed.

bath in a minute, won't we (to baby). Hello. Hello.

Oh no (at something unseen). You can really grip, can't you (to baby)? Ah (injection). A horrible stingy one.

I told you, didn't I?

Look at this baby—there (baby gripping father's finger).

Did he seem to hold your finger?

Yes, he did. Missed it before. (laughs) Oh dear.

Did he?

He wants to open his mouth— look. We will see if we can give him a feed in a minute.

Would you like to give him to his father?

(mother gives baby to father)

Oh, he doesn't like being held by me. Look—he's pulling horrible faces.

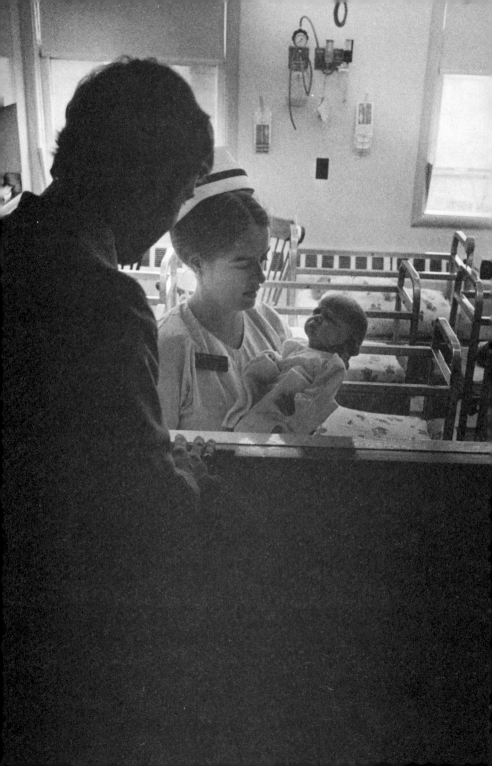

7 / Mother and Child: Separation

One puzzling question about the mother's and baby's behavior after birth is whether there really is the special and unique relationship between them that is known as attachment or bonding. The idea that such a relationship might exist and can be studied arose from animal-behavior work and from the studies of the English psychiatrist John Bowlby of the effects on institutionalized children of physical separation from their parents.

Over the last few years, psychological approaches to this question have developed in several ways. One is to inquire into the much broader area of the baby's social relationships with the world in general, and I will discuss this in the next chapter. Another is to look into the effects of separation in greater detail: Does separating mother and baby after birth interfere with early relationships in such a way as to affect their behavior when they are reunited?

The most common form of separation following birth occurs when a baby has to go into a special-care unit away from his mother. If such a separation does seem to have an adverse effect, then obviously it should be as brief as it can be made, and only where absolutely necessary. Mothers and fathers should also be encouraged to see and handle their babies whenever possible while they are in special care.

Childbirth in humans, at least until a hundred years ago, often resulted in the death of either the child or the mother. During this period, in terms of the continuing survival of the human race as a whole, it would not have made sense if the mother and baby had formed an immediate and lasting tie at birth. If the mother died, then the baby would have to be able to accept some other caregiver without too much upset in his life. If the baby died, the mother would have to be able to mourn but then go on and have more children. So one would expect any special relationship between the two to develop over a period of time. This is in contrast to some species of birds where the newborn chick very rapidly learns the features of people, animals, other birds, or objects to which it is exposed, and afterward shows special behavior toward them. If in humans the relationship does develop slowly, initial separation might have only minor effects which could be compensated for later if all went well.

When babies have to go into special-care units, it is difficult to know whether effects on the behavior of mother or baby come from the separation itself or from the reasons the baby had to go into the unit (prematurity, sickness, and so on). It is therefore more useful, perhaps, to look at evidence from separations involving normal full-term babies. A great deal of the work done on very early separation has been carried out by Marshall Klaus and John Kennell.[1] In one of their studies, done in Guatemala, a group of nine mothers were given their naked babies immediately after they had left the delivery room. A second group of nine mothers and babies were separated according to the usual hospital routine. The babies in both groups were then sent to the newborn nursery for the next twelve hours and returned to their mothers for their first feeding. Observations during this feeding of the amount of maternal fondling, kissing, gazing into the baby's face, and holding him close showed that such behavior was greater among those mothers who had had early contact with their infants.

In the context of the importance of early mother-infant contact, Klaus and Kennell quote two other observations. The first is the case of an accident at an Israeli hospital, where two mothers were given each other's babies by mistake. This was only discovered two weeks later, and when efforts were made to return the babies to their proper families, it was found that each mother had become so attached to the baby she had that she did not want to change. It was the fathers who for family reasons wanted the error corrected. Second, they cite a study done in the United States with two groups of mothers who had expressed a desire to breastfeed. One group was given their babies to suckle shortly after birth, and the other did not have contact with theirs till some sixteen hours later. No mother in either group had to stop breastfeeding for physical reasons. But two months later, the mothers who had had their infants to suckle right after birth were still all breastfeeding, while of the others five out of six had stopped.

Perhaps even more interesting than these observations was a study Klaus and Kennell did themselves.[2] They studied twenty-eight mothers of normal full-term babies. Half of the group was given the traditional American contact with their babies: a glimpse of the baby shortly after birth, brief contact and identification at six to twelve hours, and then visits for twenty to thirty minutes every four hours for bottle feeds. The other fourteen mothers were given their naked babies for one hour within the first three hours and also five extra hours' contact on each afternoon for three days after delivery. These mothers therefore had a total of an extra sixteen hours' contact with their babies.

At one month the mothers and babies returned to the hospital for three separate observations: an interview, a period of observation of each mother as her baby was being examined by a pediatrician, and a period of observation as the mother fed her baby. The mothers who had had the extra sixteen hours of extended contact showed a greater tendency to pick their babies up when they cried, though the babies were not hungry and had just had their diapers changed. These extended-contact mothers also stood closer to the baby as he was being examined and were more likely to soothe him if he became upset during the course of the examination. In the observations of feeding, these mothers spent significantly more time fondling their babies and holding them *en face*. At another examination after one year, the extended-contact mothers spent more time helping the doctor and soothing the child if he cried.[3] At two years, five mothers were randomly selected from each group to see how they talked to their children. The extended-contact mothers used twice as many questions, fewer words per proposition, more adjectives, and fewer commands. It therefore appears from all this that sixteen hours of extra contact at birth had an effect lasting for at least two years.

Most of the mothers in this case had little education, came from extremely poor social circumstances, and were having illegitimate children. I think that these factors may have had an influence on the prolongation of the affects. Very large longitudinal studies carried out over many years all indicate that the parents' social class is the best single indicator of what a child's physical and mental development will be by the age of twelve. In the poor social circumstances of the mothers in this study, the extra time and attention that one group received may have been enough to make a difference that continued. If the mothers had come from a middle-class background, I believe the differences found would have been compensated for by the relatively good environment the middle classes usually enjoy. There are two other studies that I think support this idea, done by Andrew Whiten in England and by Herbert Leiderman and Marjorie Seashore in the United States.[4] Both were mainly of middle-class mothers and examined the effects of separation when babies go into special care. Because of this, again we have to remember that differences in behavior of mother or baby might be due either to the separation or to the reason for the separation.

Whiten looked at one group of ten mothers and babies who had been separated after birth. The babies had gone into special care for between two and fourteen days for a variety of minor medical ailments, such as mild jaundice; they were considered to be medically normal on discharge from the unit. For comparison he took eleven other mothers and babies who had not been separated, and at intervals over the first year observed the mothers and babies from both groups in their homes.

At three weeks he asked the mothers to keep diaries with details of their baby's behavior for twenty-four hours. Dividing the day into five-minute blocks, the mothers recorded the amount of time the baby was in or out of his crib, and the time he spent crying, fussing, being held, being fed, being asleep, drowsy, or awake. Whiten found that the mothers in the separated group recorded over twice as much crying from their babies as the mothers of the nonseparated group. More detailed examination of the diaries indicated that the separated babies not only cried more frequently but also cried longer each time. The separated and nonseparated mothers intervened to stop their babies from crying, by picking them up and such, an equal amount of time over the twenty-four hours, but because the separated babies cried more frequently, their mothers intervened proportionately less.

When Whiten observed the mothers and babies at one month and two months, there were significant differences between the two groups in the amount of time mothers and babies spent looking and smiling at one another. The separated group looked and smiled less, and indeed the social smile appeared later in these babies. It could be that social behavior gradually increases the more mother and baby are in contact, and that it takes the separated mothers and babies time to catch up. The same would apply to the baby's ability to distinguish his own mother from a stranger on the basis of sight, hearing, and smell. It looks as though these abilities are learned by having experience of the mother, and if this is missing initially, then the learning will be delayed by the length of time the mother and baby are separated.

Interestingly, when Whiten observed his subjects at three and four months he found that most of the differences between the two groups had disappeared. There are two possible explanations: first, that Whiten's mothers were middle-class and the effects of their environment had made up for any differences caused by the original separation. The alternative is that, as the baby becomes able to do more complex things and to interact in more complex ways with his mother and the environment, so the effects of separation become "diluted" or find expression in other behavior. Although the later observations in Whiten's study have not yet been fully analyzed, there is evidence that there may be some truth in the latter explanation.

Leiderman and Seashore studied three groups of mothers. One group delivered premature infants who had to be admitted to the special-care unit for three weeks or more. During this time they were allowed to view their babies from the nursery window but never had a chance to touch them. A second group had premature infants who were admitted to the special-care unit, but the mothers were allowed in to touch and handle their babies in the incubators and cribs. The third group of mothers had full-term normal babies who were not separated. All mothers and babies were followed up for two years or more, and the researchers made observations of the kinds of behavior they judged to show maternal attachment: behavior involving close bodily contact between mother and baby; behavior involving more distant contact (looking, smiling); and time devoted solely to interacting with the baby but excluding direct caregiving procedures (feeding, changing). The mother's self-confidence was also assessed by means of a questionnaire.

The results showed that separation seemed to have very little effect on the time the mothers spent with their babies after discharge from the hospital. Nor did it affect the time they devoted to interacting with the babies outside the usual caregiving routines. There were, however, significant differences between those mothers who had been separated and those who had not in the amount of caressing they did and in the amount of time they held their babies close. The separated mothers scored lower, and also spent less time smiling at their babies. There were at first only minor differences between the behavior of mothers who had been allowed contact with their babies in the special-care unit and those who had no contact at all, although at one year the mothers allowed contact were touching their babies more. The questionnaires given to rate the mother's feelings showed that separation lowered self-confidence only in those mothers who were having their first baby, and even for these only at first. Assessments at one month and twelve months revealed no difference in maternal self-confidence in the three groups.

Follow-up one year from leaving the hospital showed that the effects of separation on the mothers' attitude and behavior had almost disappeared. Differences in the way the mothers behaved with their children seemed to be determined more by the baby's position in the family in relation to brothers and sisters, by the sex of the baby, and by the family's social class. At a year the mothers of first-born male infants were touching them more and giving them more attention than those mothers who had later-born or female infants.

When the children were followed up at twenty-one months, a rather different and surprising finding was made. Of twenty-two families where the mothers had premature children and no contact with them, five had got divorced; in the families with premature children who had contact, one had got divorced; in the group of mothers with no separation, there had been no divorces. Leiderman and Seashore suggest that the newborn period does have an effect, albeit nonspecific, by acting as a stress that might create trouble within the family structure. But there is a possibility that the stresses in family relationships may have been present before the baby was even born and that these stresses had contributed to the child's prematurity. Support for this idea also comes from one study done of children who had in some way been injured by their parents.[5] By comparing the group of children who had this misfortune with their brothers or sisters, it was shown that the abused children had had a higher than normal incidence of admission to special-care baby units, but their mothers had also had a significantly greater incidence of complications during the pregnancy with the abused children than with their brothers and sisters. Other work, by D. H. Stott, seems to show that stress in family relationships before a child is born may influence the chances of trouble with the baby after delivery, but the studies were done retrospectively and it is probable that the trouble with the child after birth was related to continuing upset in the parents' relationship.[6]

Leiderman's studies on separation were done with middle-class mothers, and the differences between his findings and those of Klaus and Kennell may be explained by the compensatory effects offered by a better environment. Still, the work of Klaus and Kennell suggests that, in very adverse social circumstances, a little help at an early stage may make a substantial difference in later maternal behavior.

Today, with modern pediatric care, babies who are born very small have an excellent chance of growing up into normal healthy adults. But to their mothers and fathers they must appear to be especially vulnerable at birth, and parents frequently voice their concern as wonder that such a small baby can ever grow to be normal in size. One recent report found little difference during follow-up between the mothers of premature babies and those of normal full-term babies, but the mothers of the premature baby still perceived him as being the "weak little one."

Investigators at University College Hospital in London followed up one hundred and sixty babies who weighed less than 1500 grams (3.25 pounds) at birth and therefore spent some time in special care.[7] At this hospital, every attempt was made to minimize the separation. Parents were allowed in to see, touch, hold, and care for their babies as much as conditions permitted; even brothers and sisters were allowed to visit. After discharge, most parents were found to go through the same stages. First there was the "honeymoon stage," lasting from one to three weeks, when the parents were excited and sometimes almost euphoric about the baby, whose continued existence had seemed so tenuous earlier. This phase was frequently followed by one of exhaustion, when the euphoria waned and the mothers began to complain of minor problems in managing the baby and especially in feeding. This stage might last a few days or even weeks, and sometimes ended when the baby started to smile and generally became more responsive. In the next phase the problems rapidly disappeared; the mother looked better and handled her baby with more confidence and increasing pleasure.

The researchers also found that getting fathers to come in and handle their babies in the unit had an effect similar to that found in the Swedish study mentioned in Chapter Five. Most fathers became frequent visitors to the unit and many regularly attended follow-up clinics after the babies' discharge; a few even brought the baby in without the mother. They asked many questions and were obviously involved in their child's day-to-day care. The investigators speculated as to whether in fact very low birth weight might be actually advantageous to the formation of paternal relationships, since several weeks of visiting the child in the hospital might allow the father time gradually to accept both the child and the inevitable changes in his relationship with his wife. Leiderman also notes the importance of bringing families, rather than just mothers, into the special units—he feels that the stresses of excluding one parent could have a very severe effect on family relationships, which many would say are stretched enough even after the birth of a full-term child in ideal circumstances.

Some hospitals have instituted a "nesting period," when mothers of premature babies can come back to hospital and take complete care of their babies for two or three days before going home. In one such hospital, many of the wives insisted that the facilities should be extended to husbands as well. Finally, it is worth noting that parents of premature babies, when asked what kind of help they needed and wanted, were given a choice of doctors, social workers, psychologists, family, and friends. But their first choice was other parents who had themselves been separated from their children. They were also very definite that they wanted the help to be within their home area so that they did not have to travel miles to get it.

In summary, then: for a nonspecific time after birth, there does seem to be a period in the developing relationship between mothers, fathers, and babies when separation may be detrimental. But the relationships will also be influenced by the condition of the baby, whether he is small or sick. Stresses and strains will continue for some time after the end of the separation, but on the whole and given a reasonable environment (the actual definition of this is exceedingly difficult to make, though one supposes from the studies that some middle-class families provide a bit of it), the effects will gradually disappear or become diluted. This would of course lead us to stress the importance not only of ensuring that the child gets the benefits of medical aid while in hospital but also of at least being aware of the influences of his social environment when he gets home. It is possible that an improvement of social circumstances might be of more benefit to health than all the medicine we have available.

108 / The Psychology of Childbirth

TRANSCRIPT: MRS. D, AGED 27, FIRST BABY (A GIRL)

Father	Mother	Midwife
It's a boy!	It's a girl! Oh, it's not, is it?	It's a girl!
Very nice, I got my things sorted out wrong.	Oh.	Beautiful, absolutely lovely.
	Oh.	
She's a beaut, Jo. (kisses wife)	Oh, oh. Where is it?	Here we are Jo, alright? You can have her in just a minute.
Congratulations.	What are we going to call it?	
(laughs) Bruce. We'll think of something. Well, I'd better . . .		Jo, can you put your feet down, love? If you want to, just

I wanted a boy.

Take it easy—that's it.

relax. It's a bit puddly, but don't worry about that.

It can't play rugby. Everyone said it was going to be a boy. What are we going to put her in?

Well, we've got plenty of things, haven't we? I thought we had everything.

She's a big one too.

She's a nice size, yes.

God, that was a quickie, wasn't it? What time was I?

Forty-six minutes.

What's that?

Yeah—no, I wasn't disappointed.

No, it wasn't a boy. I know what Ma will do—bitch.

No. Oh dear, oh dear.

She would even choose our boy's name.

So what? She might have wanted a little girl.

Father	Mother	Midwife
		Here you are, Jo.
	(*baby given to mother*)	
	Ah, oh (*greets baby*). What a funny face (*to baby*).	
Oh, she's got your nose. Now then.		
	What a funny creature you are.	
Right. Well, I'm going to phone.		
	No, wait (*to father*). Oh (*pain*). Just for a minute.	
OK.		
	She's just like a little bird, isn't she? Can you take that silly hat off (*referring to hospital cap worn by father*)?	
In a minute when I leave here.		
	No, not to my knowledge anyway (*whispers to baby*). What do you want (*to baby*)? Come on (*to baby*).	
		Do you want to spend a penny, Jo?
(*blows kisses to baby*)		

It's only the soft tissue afterbirth.

Funny! Yah (as placenta is delivered). It's slimy.

Yes. Is that everything?

You look like Sue (to father). It's a little girl.

What?

It's a little girl.

Yes, it's a little girl.

Oh, but we won't tell them that.

Oh, you're joking.

Everyone was so sure it would be a boy. I said that I could see you better with a girl.

So much for my work . . .

Just as well I can't see down there, I hate the sight of blood. Whoo, whoo (to the baby).

(sighs) Not in the slightest.

Are you sure?

Of course I'm sure.

This is a little bit sore, Jo. I just want to check. Jolly good, great super. Just one little episiotomy to suture.

Father	Mother	Midwife
That's it? Well, well, mere details now, mere details.		
		You should be fairly numb—that's what this injection's for. We can give you a bit more. You did incredibly well. Really great.
Listen, I think I'll go and phone. All right?		
	Don't go, please.	
What? No, I'm on the . . .		
	We haven't decided on a name yet, you silly ass.	
George, George.		
	What are we going to have?	
No, it doesn't matter, doesn't matter at the moment. We'll just say it's a girl.		
	How much does she weigh?	
		Don't know yet—we'll weigh her in a minute.
Ah, eight pounds and three ounces.		
	Wait and find out.	

She's not as big as everyone
said she would be.

(*baby taken away from mother*)

She's round the eight mark.
I'll tell you in a minute
when I've weighed her.

Eight pounds.

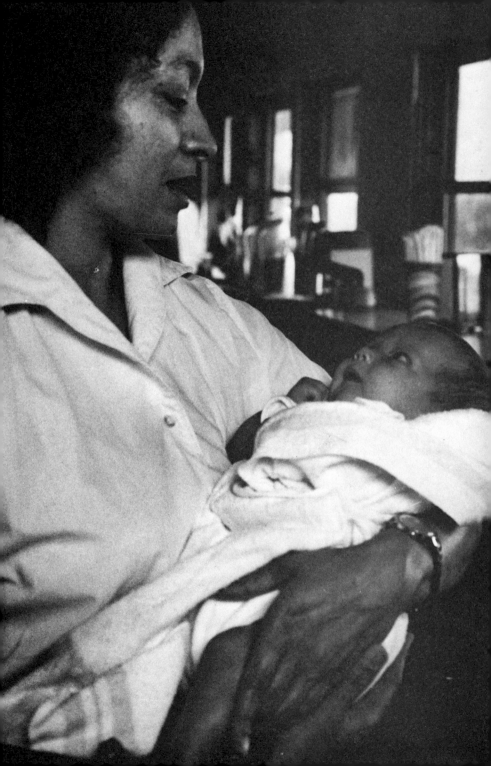

8 / Mother and Child: Socialization

At birth and during the first few days afterward, babies show a very large range of spontaneous behavior. This includes sucking and mouthing, sleeping, peeing, trying to get their hand into their mouths, smiling, erections in the male (I don't know whether anyone has looked at the female equivalent), hiccoughing, burping, defecating, moving their arms and legs, crying. There are also forms of behavior which are more directly responses to changes in the environment, such as following faces with the eyes, turning the head toward a sound, withdrawing the leg when the heel is pricked, startling at loud noises, quieting down when held.

Observations of these kinds of behavior in newborns have been made by many different investigators, and the general conclusion has been that each baby is moderately consistent in the behavior he shows over the first days of life—but that there is a great variation between individual babies in the amount of each kind they show. Thus Baby Jane, if she is good at following peoples' faces with her eyes on the third day after birth, is likely to be good at this on day ten, but over this period she might be consistently inaccurate in getting her hand into her mouth. Baby David may not look at faces over this period but be consistently able to suck on his fingers. No one yet knows exactly what factors are responsible for this variation between babies.

But variation or no, it has been suggested that there are certain features that are universally attractive to mothers in the period immediately after birth. These might include the baby's helplessness, his cry, or his physical appearance. Irenaus Eibl-Eibesfeldt had emphasized some of the unique qualities of the human baby:

the large forehead, small face, large eyes, chubby cheeks, small mouth, and unequal proportions (the baby's head is large at birth compared to his body).[1]

An experiment to see what constituted "babyish" proportions was done by B. Garner and L. Wallach using silhouettes of adult heads, baby heads, and "super-baby" heads with accentuated foreheads and smaller chins than normal.[2] These were shown to a series of American college students who, asked to pick out the one they thought most babyish, showed a consistent tendency to choose the super-baby silhouettes; this tendency was stronger among the women students than among the men. Eibl-Eibesfeldt has also done studies in different cultures in an attempt to show that the pattern of a baby's smile is the same in all children, and also that it is interpreted the same way in all cultures.[3] It does seem from his evidence that the pattern of the smile is universal, but it seems likely that the interpretation of its meaning must be different, not only in different cultures but according to the individual circumstances at particular moments.

Not all mothers like certain characteristics of a baby at birth. Some films of mothers with their babies in the delivery room immediately after birth show them turning away from the baby in disgust, with such remarks as "Oh no" or "Oh God, it looks just like its father." Howard Moss and K. S. Robson found in one of their studies that most of the women described feelings of strangeness and unfamiliarity toward their babies which persisted for at least the first few weeks of life.[4] Asked when she first felt love, when she ceased feeling strange with her child, and when the baby first became a person to her, a mother's answer frequently involved the baby's "looking" as if he were recognizing objects in his surroundings.

In one of my studies I asked ninety-seven mothers who had delivered their first babies two months previously when they first felt love for their infants. For forty it was during pregnancy, for twenty-three it was at birth, for twenty-six it was during the first week, and for eight it was some time after the end of the first week. I also asked the same mothers whether they thought that their love became stronger at any particular stage and, if so, when. Thirty thought their love grew greater at birth, twenty-nine during the first two weeks, and ten during the second two weeks. Twenty-eight thought that their love did not grow greater. There is great variation here, and it suggests that for many women the development of maternal love is a fairly gradual affair.

I have proposed earlier that one reason for a gradually developing relationship between mother and baby is that there used to be a very high deathrate at birth. Another partial explanation might be that affection between two people has to be based on learning specific characteristics of the other person. Initially one's response may be a reaction to some general feature of another but, as time goes on, the reaction may only occur when the feature is singled out as belonging individually to that one person.

Our knowledge of the mother's part in the developing relationship is taken a step further by John Newson, in a paper with the deliberately ambiguous title "Towards a Theory of Infant Understanding."[5] He proposes that "the human infant is preprogrammed to emit 'signals' and that these signals are of such a kind that his mother will inevitably pay attention to them. She is equally bound to endow them with social significance." This comes back to the observations I made of mothers with their babies in the delivery room immediately after birth; I found that in some cases the mother was even then putting social connotations on the baby's actions—something also found by H. S. Bennett in the United States, when he made a detailed study of the course of development in three infants during the first weeks of life.[6] He proposes from his observations that the caregivers (and in this case they were nurses, since the babies were going to be fostered out) use the facial expressions and spontaneous behavior of a baby to construct a fantasy about his personality, and then use this fantasy personality as the basis for handling the infant. For instance, one baby who stopped crying whenever he was picked up was seen by the nurse as "socially responsive," and another baby showing similar behavior was regarded by his nurse as "exploitative and spoilt." The first baby received maximal individual attention, and the second was left to cry.

In the words of Newson, "Human babies become human beings because they are treated as if they were human beings."[7] It would perhaps be possible to take that statement a step further: "Human babies become the type of human being they grow up to be only because they were treated like that kind of human being." At birth and even before, however, a baby has developed in such a way as to create the basis for social existence. He responds more to human beings than to objects, is more likely to turn his head toward a human voice than to a bell, and is more likely to look at a human face than at a flashing light. So just as the biology and biochemistry of the baby have developed by birth so that he is capable of breathing the oxygen from the atmosphere that surrounds him, so he has also developed in biological and biochemical ways that will allow him to live in a world of social relationships. This social milieu is one that the human organism has adapted to over millions of years, just as much as it has to the atmosphere. However, unlike the specific oxygen content of the air, social relationships are extremely variable.

The development of socialization in the first two weeks or so can take on the form of preferential behavior toward the mother as opposed to strangers. What processes of learning are involved, and how do they work?

First I would like to indicate how they do not work. It was proposed by Konrad Lorenz that the term "imprinting" should be used to apply to the special kind of learning found in many species of birds shortly after hatching. These newborn birds could respond socially to a surprising range of objects and would attempt to nestle against animals, moving boxes, flashing lights, or anything else that happened to be present at the moment after hatching. As a result of imprinting on an object, the young birds came to prefer it to other objects and eventually would come to direct their social behavior exclusively toward the familiar object. Work done by Patrick Bateson with chicks has led him to some further conclusions about the learning processes that occur in imprinting.[8] He confirmed that the development of a preference for a familiar object began in the chick at a very early stage in life, but that it lasted only until the bird became more familiar with its environment. Before the learning began, the chicks would work actively to present themselves with an object from which they could learn, and during learning they would work to present themselves with different views of the object to which they were becoming attached. Bateson also found that the preference for one object over another lasted longer or shorter according to how long the chicks were exposed to the object initially.

The term "imprinting" has been loosely used to cover many different types of behavior in many different species, but in the way that it was used originally the phenomenon has not been shown to occur in humans. This is perhaps just as well, for if human infants did show a form of imprinting, by which they begin to display specific behavior toward the first object or person they have experience of immediately after birth, it is likely that this behavior would be directed to the masked faces of the medical attendants, with unfortunate implications for later development.

Although human babies do show different behavior toward their own mothers as against strangers, this does not appear to occur immediately after birth, and in any case is only a very small variation in the baby's total repertoire of behavior. This is indicated in a study done by Louis Sander and his colleagues, who arranged for a group of babies to be looked after by one nurse in a rooming-in situation for the first ten days of life (all these babies were eventually going to be fostered).[9] The babies were fed on a self-demand feeding schedule from the first twenty-four hours. At ten days, an unfamiliar though highly experienced nurse took over the care of each child, again in the rooming-in situation. This resulted in specific disturbances in each baby's behavior, especially in the patterning of his periods of activity and sleep and crying, showing by small changes in the amount and timing of certain actions that he knew his caregiver was different.

Bateson did feel, from his work with chicks, that there were two issues relevant to humans. First, certain stages of development are crucial for the acquisition of preferences and habits. Second, the young are far from being passive little creatures but play an active part in determining the kind of stimulation they get. The first of these issues has obvious implications for mother-child separation. It seems possible that there is a sensitive period in humans immediately after birth for the development of relations between mother and child, and that this could get upset by separation, at least in the short term. The second issue is more complicated. As a newborn child does seem to show preferential responses toward people rather than objects, he is to a degree playing an active part in the type of stimulation he is getting. However, a chick is born feathered and mobile, and this mobility gives it the chance of seeking out its stimulation. The human newborn can only attempt to call the stimulation to himself by crying, and then try and hold it there.

But how much do the infant and the mother influence one another's behavior? David Levy, in a series of observations of mother-newborn relationships, looked at mothers' greeting response when their babies were brought in by a nurse the first two or three times after birth.[10] He found that there was great variation in these greetings and that a mother who greeted her baby on one occasion might not do so on another. Mothers rated as very maternal seemed no different in this respect from those rated as not very maternal at all. It seemed that the greeting depended mainly on the baby's behavior. On those occasions when he was quiet and awake, the mother always greeted him, but when he was crying she greeted him only about once in three times and when he was asleep only once in six. Levy felt that it was possible to infer devotion, interest, affection, tenderness, and that it was possible just to conjecture that there was an underlying feeling of possession, as of having something highly treasured. It is also possible to infer from the study that the mother's behavior is very much dependent on that of her baby, and that simple observations of a mother's behavior could be grossly misleading about her actual feelings. Levy also found that to some extent the mothers' behavior was a result of how they expected a situation to develop. Thus he found that the mother's anticipation of the problems of feeding served to curtail her greeting.

Work by Louis Sander also indicates how baby and mother each start off acting fairly autonomously, without at first synchronizing their behavior, and only gradually over the weeks adapt to one another's routines.[11] He had three groups of nine babies in three different situations. Group 1 spent the first ten days in a nursery and then were roomed-in with one of two nurses, X or Y, for eighteen days before being fostered out. Group 2 was roomed-in with a nurse for ten days, changed to another nurse for eighteen days, and then fostered out (this group I have already mentioned). Finally, babies in Group 3 were roomed-in with their mothers for five days, and then went home with the mothers and were with them thereafter.

Many fascinating findings emerge from this study. For instance, when the babies in Group 1, who had been in the nursery, were given to the nurses on day ten, those with Nurse Y began to cry less, while those given to Nurse X continued as before. When Sander looked at the behavior of the nurses to discover what might be responsible for the difference, he found that Nurse X followed very simple, nowadays generally held precepts of infant care, including demand feeding. She had the feeling that all that was required was to love the babies. Although she perceived individual differences between the infants in her care, she did not often draw on this information to vary her method of dealing with them. Nurse Y, on the other hand, was always using her keen ability to perceive individual differences and trying out different ways of caregiving which these differences might specifically require from her. "In other words her aim was in the direction of establishing unique interactions upon which stability in an individual infant's course would become predictable for her."

The Sander study also revealed much else of interest. From the activity records of individual babies it appears that some children in the first few days of life show recurrent peaks of activity every three to five hours within a twenty-four-hour span. These periods of activity at first hardly coincide at all with the periods of caregiving activity. But by the fifteenth day the times of peak activity have lost their periodicity, while sleep periods have grown longer and tend to gather at night. At the same time, the baby's periods of activity and the caregiving activity have become more synchronized, suggesting that in the ten to fifteen days following birth the baby and his caregiver are beginning to get themselves coordinated.

Theodore Gaensbauer set out to discover whether the distribution of awake, alert periods relative to feeds was different for demand-fed babies than for schedule-fed ones.[12] He found that the total amount of wakefulness in the two groups was very much the same, which suggested that "there may be intrinsic mechanisms which regulate the proportionate amounts of time an infant will spend in sleep and wakefulness." However, the distribution of the periods of alertness was indeed different. Demand-fed infants showed little wakefulness during the feeding and for most of the time between feeds, except for a period of high alertness just before each feed began. The schedule-fed babies had their wakefulness spread less unevenly, since almost all of it occurred just before or after feeds. It is worth noting in passing that the demand-fed group appeared to have an intrinsic sleep-wake cycle, which ran over approximately four hours.

A large number of recent studies have looked at the behavior of mothers and babies together in detail. Some of this work was pioneered by Martin Richards, and his examination, frame by frame, of films taken of mothers and babies smiling at one another shows a very precise sequencing of behavior between the two partners.[13] For instance, a mother would smile at her baby, and the baby would watch with close attention; when she stopped smiling, the baby's activity would increase and at the moment of maximum "pumped-upness" he would smile; if during this period the mother did not stop all her own activity to let the baby do his smile, he would get upset and fretful.

With Judy Bernal, Richards has more recently been doing detailed observations of babies in the period around birth to see how a mother's behavior influences her baby's and vice-versa.[14] They found that one particular aspect of feeding was different: among bottle-feeding mothers it was usually the mother who pulled the nipple from the baby's mouth; among breastfeeders, the feeds were ended just as often by the baby's releasing the nipple. Richards and Bernal also found that kissing, rocking, and affectionate touching were more common with breastfeeders, while rubbing, patting, jiggling, and concern about bringing up gas predominated among bottle-feeders.

When observing infants and mothers together it is frequently difficult to tell who starts a sequence and who ends it. For instance, on one of Andrew Whiten's videotapes of a feed, a mother who was holding her child to the breast with one hand under his neck suddenly reached for a cloth. About five seconds later, the child vomited and the mother had the cloth ready by his mouth. Looking at the videotape there was no way to tell how she had known in advance that the baby was going to vomit. When we played the tape back to this mother, she explained that she had felt the muscles tighten in the back of his neck, and she knew from previous experience what that forecast.

This kind of detail on the interactive behavior of mother and child can give us clues as to how a fetus actually does develop into a social being. Perhaps psychologists are attempting to be modern-day prophets, taking over from the astrologers of yesterday.

Epilogue

If I have any one strong belief after reviewing the research and my own experiences, it is that childbirth is, in the main, a normal physiological process that might be enhanced if women felt, and were encouraged to feel, competent at it and confident in themselves and their bodies.

It seems a pity that in our society success and social status are so often associated with the immediate acquirement of money. With this, the position of women in childbearing and childrearing, which now (although not always in the past) brings little financial reward, has been relegated to a secondary position. The French, ever realistic, give benefits to parents of between $1200 and $1800 if they attend an antenatal clinic and bring the child for regular checkups over the first year of his life. Where concern for the child's actual health may not motivate them to come to the clinics, financial reward does. (This was also a far-sighted investment in economic terms, for high attendance at the clinics has reduced the incidence of death and handicap, and the government has to spend less on the provision of special homes and facilities.)

I also think it necessary to remember that the system of reproduction developed as a whole, as part of a larger biological system. Its features did not evolve independently. It is not just that mothers developed to be specially good at looking after babies or babies to be specially attractive to their mothers. They are both part of a system designed to make sure that children will grow into adults, and reproduce in turn, thus enabling the species to continue. It is not just the child's relationship with his mother that matters, but his relationships with his mother, father, other human beings, and the environment in general.

Finally I am aware that the book covers only a few facets of the relationship between an infant and his environment before, during, and after birth and between a mother and her baby. It could hardly deal with all the interdependent behavior and feelings that occur twenty-four hours a day and seven days a week. Nor can it give any idea of how stressful and demanding this involvement is. At best I have sketched in one or two marks on a huge, intricate, and varied canvas, knowing that the whole will always be far more than the constituent parts and that the picture can never be finished.

References
Suggested Reading
Index

References

1 Life Before Birth

1. L. Watson, *Supernature* (London: Hodden and Stoughton, 1973).
2. L. W. Sontag and R. F. Wallce, "The Effect of Cigarette Smoking During Pregnancy upon Fetal Heart Rate," *American Journal of Obstetrics and Gynecology*, 1935, *29*, 77-82. L. W. Sontag and R. F. Wallace, "The Movement Response of the Human Fetus to Sound Stimuli," *Child Development*, 1935, *6*, 253-258.
3. F. E. Hytten, "Metabolic Adaptation of Pregnancy in the Prevention of Handicap Through Antenatal Care." In A. C. Turnbull and F. P. Woodford, eds., *Review of Research Practice*, *18* (Amsterdam: Elsevier, 1976).
4. L. W. Sontag, "Changes in the Rate of the Human Fetal Heartbeat in Response to Vibratory Stimuli," *American Journal of the Diseases of Childhood*, 1936, *51*, 583-589.
5. J. C. Grimwade et al., "Human Fetal Heartrate Change and Movement in Response to Sound and Vibration," *American Journal of Obstetrics and Gynecology*, 1971, *109*, 86-90.
6. D. Walker et al., "Intrauterine Noise, a Component of the Fetal Environment," *American Journal of Obstetrics and Gynecology*, 1971, *109*, 91-95.
7. L. Salk, "The Role of the Heartbeat in the Relationship Between Mother and Infant," *Scientific American*, March 1973.
8. L. W. Sontag, "Implications of Fetal Behavior and Environment for Adult Personalities," *Annals of the New York Academy of Science*, 1966, *134(2)*, 782.

2 Social and Psychological Factors

1. Office of Population Censuses and Surveys, *Classification of Occupations* (London: HMSO, 1976).
2. E. C. Mann, "The Role of Emotional Determinants in Habitual Abortion," *Surgical Clinics of North America*, 1959, *37*, 447.
3. S. Rosen, "Emotional Factors in Nausea and Vomiting of Pregnancy," *Psychiatric Quarterly*, 1955, *29*, 621.
4. A. Blau et al., "The Psychogenic Etiology of Premature Births," *Psychosomatic Medicine*, 1963, *25*, 201.
5. A. Coppen, "Psychosomatic Aspects of Pre-Eclamptic Toxemia,"

Journal of Psychosomatic Research, 1958, *2,* 241-265.
6. H. Bakow et al., "The Relation Between Newborn Behaviour and Mother-Child Interaction" (Paper presented at Society for Research in Child Development, March 1973).
7. P. A. Chapple and W. D. Furneaux, "Changes of Personality in Pregnancy and Labour," *Proceedings of the Royal Society of Medicine,* 1964, *57,* 260-261.
8. D. Breen, *The Birth of a First Child* (London: Tavistock Publications, 1975).
9. A. J. Ferreira, "The Pregnant Mother's Emotional Attitude and Its Reflection upon the Newborn," *American Journal of Orthopsychiatry,* 1960, *30,* 553-561.
10. L. W. Sontag, "The Significance of Fetal Environmental Differences," *American Journal of Obstetrics and Gynecology,* 1941, *42,* 996-1003.

3 The Delivery: When and Where

1. H. F. R. Prechtl, "Behavioural State Cycles in Abnormal Infants," *Developmental Medicine and Child Neurology,* 1973, *15,* 606-615.
2. K. Greene, "The Psychological Effects on Women of the Induction of Labour" (unpublished dissertation, University of Cambridge, 1974).
3. S. Kitzinger, "Some Mothers' Experiences of Induced Labour" (submission to the Department of Health and Social Security from the National Childbirth Trust, 1975).
4. Kitzinger, "Some Mothers' Experiences of Induced Labour."
5. G. J. Kloosterman, "Obstetrics in the Netherlands: A Survival or a Challenge?" (paper presented at Tunbridge Wells Meeting on Problems in Obstetrics organized by the Medical Information Unit of the Spastics Society, 1975).
6. N. Newton, "Mice Delivery in Known and Unfamiliar Environments" (paper presented to the Nineteenth Congress of Psychology, London, 1969).

4 Pain and Relief

1. M. Mead and N. Newton, "Cultural Patterning of Perinatal Behavior." In S. A. Richardson and A. F. Guttmacher, eds., *Childbearing, Its Social and Psychological Aspects* (Baltimore: Williams and Wilkins, in press).
2. E. Marais, *The Soul of the Ape* (Harmondsworth: Penguin, 1973).
3. P. J. Tomlin, "Pethidine Compared with Pethidine Plus Levall-

orphan, and Sterile Water," *British Journal of Anaesthesia*, 1965, *37*, 23-28.

4. L. Chertok, *Psychosomatic Methods in Painless Childbirth* (Oxford: Pergamon Press, 1959).

5. J. W. Scanlon, "Neurobehavioral Responses of Newborn Infants after Maternal Epidural Anesthesia," *Anesthesiology*, 1974, *40*(2), 121-128.

6. P. J. Tomlin, "Pethidine Compared with Pethidine Plus Levallorphan, and Sterile Water."

7. T. B. Brazelton, "Effect of Prenatal Drugs on the Behavior of the Neonate," *American Journal of Psychiatry*, 1973, *126*, 1261-1266.

8. G. Stechler, "Newborn Attention as Affected by Medication During Labour," *Science*, 1964, *144*, 315-317.

9. Y. Brackbill et al., "Obstetric Meperidine Usage and Assessment of Neonatal Status," *Anesthesiology*, 1974, *40*, 116-120. E. Carway and Y. Brackbill, "Delivery Medication and Infant Outcome: An Empirical Study." In W. A. Bowes et al., eds., *Effects of Obstetrical Medication on the Fetus and Infant* (Monograph of the Society for Research in Child Development No. 35, 1970).

10. M. P. M. Richards and J. F. Bernal, "An Observational Study of Mother-Infant Interaction." In N. Blurton Jones, ed., *Ethological Studies of Child Behaviour* (New York and Cambridge: Cambridge University Press, 1974).

11. S. Turner and J. A. Macfarlane, "Auditory Localization in the Newborn Infant and the Effects of Pethidine," *Developmental Medicine and Child Neurology* (in press).

12. G. Dick-Read, *Childbirth Without Fear* (first published 1933; London: Heinemann Medical Books, 1968; 4th ed., New York: Harper and Row, 1972).

13. S. Kitzinger, *The Experience of Childbirth*, 3rd ed. (Harmondsworth and New York: Penguin, 1972).

14. Chertok, *Psychosomatic Methods in Painless Childbirth*.

5 The First Minutes

1. H. M. Klaus and J. Kennell, "Human Maternal Behaviour at First Contact with Her Young," *Pediatrics*, 1970, *46*(2), 187-192.

2. K. S. Robson and H. A. Moss, "Patterns and Determinants of Maternal Attachment," *Journal of Pediatrics*, 1970, *77*, 976-985.

3. J. Grey, C. Cutler, J. Dean, and C. H. Kempe, "The Denver Predictive Study from the National Center for the Prevention and Treatment of Child Abuse and Neglect" (unpublished paper, University of Colorado Medical Center).

4. M. Wertheimer, "Psychomotor Coordination of Auditory-Visual

Space at Birth," *Science*, 1961, *134*, 1692.
5. F. Leboyer, *Birth Without Violence* (New York: Alfred A. Knopf, 1975; London: Wildwood House, 1975).
6. W. J. Henneborn and R. Cogan, "The Effect of Husband Participation on Reported Pain and the Probability of Medication During Labour and Birth," *Journal of Psychosomatic Research*, 1975, *19*, 215-222.
7. M. Greenberg and N. Morris, "Engrossment: A Newborn's Impact on the Father," *Journal of Orthopsychiatry*, 1974, *44*, 520-531.

6 What the Baby Knows

1. P. H. Wolff, "Observations on the Development of Smiling." In B. M. Foss, ed., *Determinants of Infant Behaviour*, 2 (London: Methuen, 1963).
2. H. F. R. Prechtl and D. Beintema, "Neurological Examination of the Full-Term Newborn Infant," *Clinics in Developmental Medicine No. 12* (London: Spastics International Medical Publications and Heinemann, 1964). S. J. Hutt et al., "Influence of 'State' upon Responsivity to Stimulation." In S. J. Hutt and C. Hutt, eds., *Early Human Development* (Oxford: Oxford University Press, 1973).
3. J. A. Macfarlane and P. Harris, "Central and Peripheral Vision in Early Infancy," *Journal of Experimental Psychology*, 1976, *21(3)*, 532-538.
4. H. F. R. Prechtl, "Problems of Behavioural Studies in the Newborn Infant." In D. S. Lehoman, R. A. Hinde, and E. Shaw, eds., *Advances in the Study of Behaviour* (New York and London: Academic Press, 1965).
5. R. L. Fantz, "The Origins of Form Perception," *Scientific American*, 1961, *204*, 66-72.
6. R. L. Fantz et al., "Early Visual Selectivity." In L. B. Cohen and P. Salapatek, eds., *Infant Perception: From Sensation to Cognition*, 1 (New York and London: Academic Press, 1975).
7. A. M. Slater and J. M. Findlay, "Binocular Fixation in the Newborn," *Journal of Experimental Child Psychology*, 1975, *20*, 248.
8. T. G. R. Bower, *Development in Infancy* (San Francisco: W. H. Freeman, 1974).
9. G. Carpenter, "Mother's Face and the Newborn," *New Scientist*, 21 March 1974, 742-744.
10. M. Wertheimer, "Psychomotor Coordination of Auditory-Visual Space at Birth," *Science*, 1961, *134*, 1692.
11. S. J. Hutt, "Auditory Discrimination at Birth." In S. J. Hutt and C. Hutt, eds., *Early Human Development*.

12. M. Mills, "Recognition of Mother's Voice in Early Infancy," *Nature*, 1974.
13. X. Turkewitz et al., "Effects of Intensity of Auditory Stimulation on Directional Eye Movements in the Human Neonate," *Animal Behaviour*, 1966, *14*, 93-101.
14. W. Condon, "Speech Makes Babies Move," *New Scientist*, 6 June 1974, 624-627.
15. T. Engen, L. P. Lipsitt, and H. Kay, "Olfactory Responses and Adaptation in the Human Neonate," *Journal of Comparative Physiology and Psychology*, 1963, *56*, 3-5.
16. J. A. Macfarlane, "Olfaction in the Development of Social Preferences in the Human Neonate." In *Parent-Infant Interaction* (Amsterdam: CIBA Foundation Symposium 33, new series, ASP, 1975).
17. K. Crook and L. P. Lipsitt, "Neonatal Nutritive Sucking: Effects of Taste Stimulation upon Sucking Rhythm and Heart Rate," *Child Development*, 1976, *47*, 518-522.
18. P. Johnson and D. M. Salisbury, "Breathing and Sucking During Feeding in the Newborn." In *Parent-Infant Interaction* (Amsterdam: CIBA Foundation Symposium 33, new series, ASP, 1975).
19. J. F. Bernal, "Crying During the First Ten Days and Maternal Responses," *Developmental Medicine and Child Neurology*, 1972, *14*, 362.
20. M. P. M. Richards, J. F. Bernal, and Y. Brackbill, "Early Behavioural Differences: Gender or Circumcision," *Developmental Psychobiology*, 1976, *9*, 89-95.
21. J. A. Ambrose, discussion contribution in J. A. Ambrose, ed., *Stimulation in Early Infancy* (New York and London: Academic Press, 1970).

7 Mother and Child: Separation

1. H. J. Kennell et al., "Evidence for a Sensitive Period in the Human Mother." In *Parent-Infant Interaction* (Amsterdam: CIBA Foundation Symposium 33, new series, ASP, 1975).
2. M. Klaus et al., "Maternal Attachment: Importance of the First Post-Partum Days," *New England Journal of Medicine*, 1972, *286*, 460.
3. H. J. Kennell et al., "Maternal Behaviour One Year after Early and Extended Post Partum Contact," *Developmental Medicine and Child Neurology*, 1974, *16*(2), 172-179.
4. A. Whiten, "Postnatal Separation and Mother-Infant Interaction" (paper presented at the Conference of the International Society for the Study of Behavioural Development, University of Surrey,

1975). M. J. Seashore et al., "The Effects of Denial of Early Mother-Infant Interaction on Maternal Self-Confidence," *Journal of Personality and Social Psychology*, 1973 *26*(3), 369-378.

5. A. M. Lynch, "Ill-Health and Child Abuse," *The Lancet*, 16 August 1975, 317.

6. D. H. Scott, "Follow-up Study from Birth of the Effects of Prenatal Stresses," *Developmental Medicine and Child Neurology*, 1973, *15*, 770-787.

7. A. Blake, A. Stewart, and D. Turcan, "Parents of Babies of Very Low Birth Weight." In *Parent-Infant Interaction*.

8 Mother and Child: Socialization

1. I. E. Eibl-Eibesfeldt, *Love and Hate* (London: Methuen, 1971).

2. B. Garner and L. Wallach, "Shapes of Figures Identified as a Baby's Head," *Perceptual and Motor Skills*, 1965, *20*, 135-142.

3. I. E. Eibl-Eibesfeldt, *Ethology: The Biology of Behavior* (New York: Holt, Rinehart and Winston, 1970).

4. K. S. Robson and H. A. Moss, "Patterns and Determinants of Maternal Attachment," *Journal of Pediatrics*, 1970, *77*, 976-985.

5. J. Newson, "Towards a Theory of Infant Understanding," *Bulletin of the British Psychological Society*, 1974, *27*, 251-257.

6. H. S. Bennett, "Infant-Caretaker Interactions," *Journal of American Child Psychiatry*, 1971, *10*(2).

7. Newson, "Towards a Theory of Infant Understanding."

8. P. P. G. Bateson, "The Imprinting of Birds." In S. A. Barnett, ed., "Ethology and Development," *Clinics in Developmental Medicine No. 47* (London: Spastics International Medical Publications and Heinemann, 1973).

9. L. S. Sander et al., "Early Mother-Infant Interaction and Twenty-Four-Hour Patterns of Activity and Sleep," *Journal of the American Academy of Child Psychiatry*, 1970, *9*, 103.

10. D. Levy, *Behavioral Analysis* (Springfield, Ill.: Thomas, 1958).

11. Sander et al., "Early Mother-Infant Interaction and Twenty-Four-Hour Patterns of Activity and Sleep."

12. T. J. Gaensbauer and R. N. Emde, "Wakefulness and Feeding in Human Newborns," *Archives of General Psychiatry*, 1973, *28*, 894-897.

13. H. R. Schaffer, ed., *Interactions in Infancy* (New York and London: Academic Press, in press).

14. J. F. Bernal, "Consistency and Change in Maternal Style." In *Parent-Infant Interaction* (Amsterdam: CIBA Foundation Symposium 33, new series, ASP, 1975).

Suggested Reading

Dana Breen, *The Birth of a First Child* (London: Tavistock Publications, 1975). Interesting but fairly complex and technical results of an in-depth psychological examination of fifty women experiencing late pregnancy and early motherhood for the first time; worth the effort it demands.

Geraldine Flanagan, *The First Nine Months of Life* (New York: Simon and Schuster, 1962; London: Heinemann Medical Books, 1963). A fairly detailed account of how the fetus develops in the uterus. It includes a number of color photos of fetuses at different stages, together with sequences of shots showing movement in response to touch.

Sheila Kitzinger, *The Experience of Childbirth*, 3rd ed. (Harmondsworth and New York: Penguin, 1972). A fine and very popular introduction to Sheila Kitzinger's own method of preparation for birth, which involves not only understanding of the physiology of birth and acquaintanceship with relaxation and breathing techniques, but also acceptance of birth as part of a woman's sexual development.

Sheila Kitzinger and John Davies, eds., *The Place of Birth* (Oxford: Oxford University Press, in press). A fascinating collection of papers on the advantages and disadvantages of home and hospital delivery. Not particularly easy to read but an important book.

Raven Lang, *The Birth Book* (Palo Alto, Calif.: Science and Behavior Books, 1972). Some fascinating descriptions by a group of people involved, despite legal prohibition, in home deliveries in the state of California. The book shows some of the alternatives open to people with this kind of determination.

Frederick Leboyer, *Birth Without Violence* (New York: Alfred A. Knopf, 1975; London: Wildwood House, 1975). The rationale behind this French obstetrician's novel approach to delivery; brief, illustrated, distinctly poetic for a book on this topic, and certainly rather compelling.

Roger Lewin, ed., *Child Alive* (New York: Doubleday, 1975; London: Temple-Smith, 1975). A substantial collection of extremely readable articles by a number of leading researchers in child development; an excellent introduction to the surprising competence of small babies.

M. P. M. Richards, ed., *The Integration of the Child into a Social World* (Cambridge: Cambridge University Press, 1974). Another collection of papers, but at a much higher level. It raises a number of tough but interesting issues concerned with the question of how human beings become social.

Index

Acupuncture, for relief of pain in childbirth, 37, 43
Age differences: in fetal response to touch, 10; in response to light, 12
Ambrose, Anthony, 88-89
Anesthesia, of mother, 40
Animals: environmental effects on labor of, 30-31; birth pains among, 34; behavior of immediately after birth, 53
Anxiety, effects of in mother, 18, 20-21
Attachment, or bonding, 99

Baby: experience of birth for, 56-58; behavior of as determinant of socialization, 119-120; synchronization with mother, 121-122. See also Fetus; Newborn
Bakow, Harry, 18, 20
Barbiturates, 38-39
Bateson, Patrick, 118
Bennett, H. S., 117
Bernal, Judy, 86
Biochemical changes in mother, 17
Biological factors, and social class, 17
Birthrate, decrease in, 23
Bower, Tom, 78
Bowlby, John, 99
Brackbill, Yvonne, 39
Brazelton, T. Berry, 38
Breastfeeding: vs. bottle-feeding, 85-86, 122; length of, 100-101
Breathing movements of fetus, 11
Breene, Dana, 19
Browne, Sir Thomas, 5

Cambridge University, study of induction at, 27
Carpenter, Genevieve, 78
Cervix, state of at delivery, 25
Chapple, P. A., 19
Charing Cross Hospital, 59
Chertok, Leon, 42 *
Childbirth, "natural," 41, 125-126. See also Delivery; Mother
Chinese: age of child among, 5; prenatal clinics of, 6
Chloroform, 37
Circumcision, 86-87
Class differences: in attitudes toward childbirth, 41; in presence of father at delivery, 59; in breastfeeding, 86; in effects of separation of mother and child, 101-102. See also Social class
Cogan, R., 60
Coleridge, Samuel Taylor, 5
Condon, William, 81
Coppen, A., 18

da Vinci, Leonardo, 6
Davies, John, 31, 56
Deathrate: for babies at birth, 16; consequences of lower, 23; in Holland, 29; effects of, 99-100, 117
Delivery: place of, 23-24; use of induction, 24-28; home vs. hospital, 29-31
Depression after birth, 30
Dick-Read, Grantly, 41
Drugs: influence of on fetus, 6, 17, 38-39; for inducing labor, 25; for relief of pain, 37-40, 54; in psychoprophylaxis, 42
Dunn, Judy, 39

137

Eibel-Eibesfeldt, Irenäus, 115-116
Engen, T., 82
Epidural anesthesia, 37-38
Ether, 37
Eye movements of newborn: in tracking, 76; connected with sound, 79-81

Fantz, Robert, 76
Fathers: presence of at delivery, 54, 58-60; visits of to premature babies, 106
Ferreira, A. J., 20
Fetus: effects of interaction with mother, 6-7; effects of sound on, 7-9; movements of, 9-12; seeing by, 12; ability to taste, 84. See also Newborn
Fisher, C., 37
France, checks on infants' health in, 125
Furneaux, W. D., 19

Gaensbauer, Theodore, 121
Garner, B., 116
Great Britain: emphasis of research in, 15; home vs. hospital for delivery in, 24, 29-30; use of drugs in childbirth, 40; presence of father at delivery, 59

Harris, Paul, 75
Hearing: of fetus, 7-9; of newborn, 79-81
Heartbeat: changes in fetal, 6; sound of maternal, 9; as response to sight, 76; to sound, 79; to smell, 82; to taste, 84; as comforting rhythm, 88-89
Henneborn, W. J., 60
Hippocrates, 5
Hirsh, X., 6
Home: as place for childbirth, 23; vs. hospital, 29-31; births in, in

Netherlands, 29
Hutt, John, 79
Hypnosis, for pain in childbirth, 36, 42
Hytten, Frank, 7

Imitation in newborns, 89
Imprinting, 118
Induction of labor: methods of, 25; merits of, 26-27; judgments of mothers on, 27-28; and presence of fathers, 59

Kay, H., 82
Kempe, Henry, 56
Kennell, John, 52, 54; on mother-child separation, 100, 101, 105
Kitzinger, Sheila, 27, 42
Klaus, Marshall, 52, 54; on mother-child separation, 100, 101, 105
Kloosterman, G. J., 29

Labor: and maternal anxiety, 18, 20-21; induction of, 24-28
Lamaze, Fernand, 41
Leboyer, Frederick, 57-58
Leiderman, Herbert, 102, 103-104, 106
Levallorphan, 38
Levy, David, 120
Lipsitt, L. P., 82, 84, 88-89
Lorenz, Konrad, 118

Malnutrition, maternal, effect of on fetus, 6, 17
Marais, Eugene, 34
Maternity Home Help, 29
Mead, Margaret, 33
Meltzov, Andrew, 89
Midwife, 6, 24, 29, 53
Mills, Margaret, 80
Miscarriage (spontaneous abortion), 17
Moss, Howard, 55-56, 116

Mother: effect of fetus on, 7; rhythmic sound in uterus of, 9; effect of emotional stress in, 11; psychology of, 17-21; effect of anxiety in, 20; behavior immediately after delivery, 51-56, 120; baby's recognition of, 80. *See also* Separation, mother-child; Socialization
Movements of fetus in uterus, 8, 9-12
Moxacombustion, 43

National Childbirth Trust, 27, 31
Nausea, and psychology of mother, 17-18
Netherlands: childbirth practices in, 29; use of drugs for childbirth in, 40
Newborn: reflexes of, 73, 88; ways of studying, 73-74; optimum time for observation, 74-75; effect of position on, 75; sight of, 76-79; hearing of, 79-81; sense of smell, 81-83; sense of taste, 83-86; ability to feel pain, 86-87; touch and temperature, 88; rhythms of, 88-89; imitation by, 89; features attractive to mothers, 115-116
Newson, John, 117
Nitrous oxide, 40

Occupation, social class by, 16
Ounstead, M., 27
Oxytocin, 25; effect of on babies, 26

Pain in childbirth: attitudes toward, 33; in animals, 34-35; physiology of, 35; psychological aspects of, 36; relief of, 37-43; of baby at birth, 56-57, 86-87; and presence of father, 60
Parents' relationship, and treatment of babies, 104-105
Periodicity, sensed by newborn, 89

Pethidine, 38, 39
Prechtl, Heinz, 26, 75
Pregnancy: abnormalities in, and psychology of mother, 17-19; psychoanalysis on, 19; as normal, 19-20, 33, 125-126; mother's anxiety in, 20
Premature babies: parental attitudes toward, 105; facilities for parental contacts with, 105-106
Prematurity, and psychology of mother, 18
Presley, Elvis, 7
Prostaglandins, 25, 27
Psychoanalysis, on pregnancy, 19
Psychological factors influencing childbirth, 15; in mother, 17-21; and pain, 35
Psychology of mother: and abnormalities in pregnancy and delivery, 17-19; and variations in normal pregnancy, 19-20; emotions and baby's behavior, 20-21
Psychoprophylaxis: Russian study of in childbirth, 36; other work on, 40-42

Reflexes, of newborn, 73, 88
Relief from pain, methods of: drugs, 37-40; psychoprophylaxis, 40-42; hypnosis, 42; acupuncture, 43
Rhythms, reaction of newborn to, 88-89
Richards, Martin, 39, 86, 122
Robson, Kenneth S., 55-56, 116
Rooting reflex: in fetus, 10; in newborn, 88
Rosen, S. S., 18

Salamander reflex, 88
Salisbury, David, 84
Salk, Lee, 9
Sander, Louis, 81, 119, 120-121
Seashore, Marjorie, 102, 103-104

Separation of mother and child: effects of, 99-107; baby into special care, 99, 100, 102; vs. early mother-child contact, 100-105; in premature babies, 105-106
Serenus, 5
Sex of child, parental reaction to, 55
Sex differences, in newborn's reaction to touch, 88
Sight of newborn, 76-79
Simpson, James Young, 37
Sleep patterns of fetus, 11
Smell, newborn's sense of, 81-83
Smoking, influence of on fetus, 6-7, 17
Snow, John, 37
Social class: influence of on childbirth, 15, 16-17; and effects of mother-child separation, 102-103
Socialization, mother and child: role of baby in, 119-120; synchronization in, 121
Sontag, L. W., 6, 11; on effects of sound on fetus, 8; on anxiety of mothers, 20
Sounds, frequencies of, 79
Soviet Union: study of pain at childbirth in, 36; use of psychoprophylaxis in, 40-41
Special-care units, 27; for premature babies, 100-106
Stechler, Gerald, 39
Stott, D. H., 105
Sucking: affected by drugs, 39; as distraction, 75
Sweden: use of drugs for childbirth in, 40; study of involvement of fathers, 60, 106

Tanzer, S., 60
Taste, newborn's sense of, 83-86
Temperature: effect on baby, 76; newborn's sense of, 88
Thalidomide, 6
Touch: fetal movement in response to, 10; newborn's sense of, 88
Toxemia, 18
Transcripts of first minutes after delivery, 44-49, 61-70, 90-97, 108-113

United States: research on childbirth in, 15; laws governing childbirth in, 24; home vs. hospital for birth in, 29-30; "natural" childbirth in, 61, 125; presence of father at delivery in, 59
University College Hospital, London, 105-106
Uterus: fetus' life in, 5-12; early notions of influences in, 6-7; sound in, 7-9; movements in, 9-12; seeing in, 12

Victoria, Queen, 37

Wales, research on childbirth in, 16, 36
Wallach, L., 116
Watson, Lyall, 5
Wertheimer, Michael, 79
Whiten, Andrew, 102-103, 122
Wolff, Peter, 74-75

X-rays, effect on fetus, 6

Credits

4   Carnegie Institute

14   George Malave (Stock/Boston)

22   Sam Sweezy (Stock/Boston)

32   George Malave (Stock/Boston)

50   Sam Sweezy (Stock/Boston)

72   Anna Kaufman Moon (Stock/Boston)

98   Frank Siteman (Stock/Boston)

114   Peter Simon (Stock/Boston)

124   Peter Simon (Stock/Boston)